HENS IN THE GARDEN, EGGS IN THE KITCHEN

Charlotte Popescu

CAVALIER PAPERBACKS

© Charlotte Popescu 2003
cover photo by the author

Published by Cavalier Paperbacks 2003
Reprinted 2003
Reprinted 2004
Reprinted 2005
Reprinted 2006
Reprinted 2007

Cavalier Paperbacks
Burnham House,
Upavon,
Wilts SN9 6DU

www.cavalierpaperbacks.co.uk

ISBN 9781899470235
ISBN 1-899470-23-9

Printed and bound in Great Britain by Cromwell Press,
White Horse Business Park, Trowbridge, Wiltshire

CONTENTS

INTRODUCTION

Around 21 million hens live in battery cages in the UK and the majority of eggs produced from all hens come from battery hens. Only around 18% are free-range. I keep bantams as pets and for their eggs and have gradually increased my flock over the years so that I have 20 hens and one cockerel. I have different pure breeds and various cross breeds and I have Tilly, (our oldest resident) a little speckly bantam bought seven years ago, a wonderful mother to several broods of chicks and still very active. We particularly like our silver-laced Wyandottes (four hens and a cock) and I hope to breed some more this year. I also have a couple of buff Sussexes, a Vorwerk hen (from a hatchable egg bought from the Domestic Fowl Trust) and some Araucana/Buff Sussex crosses who lay bluey green eggs.

When I first had bantams my husband built me a chicken hutch and we kept them enclosed in a run with a six foot fence. I tried to keep my bantams inside their run but they were forever getting out – the grass being much greener on the other side! In the end I netted all my vegetables and let them out during the day to roam the garden. They now also have a field in which to roam and they are completely free-range. Most of them roost in a coniferous tree for the night but the others sleep in hen houses. They are a happy bunch and, because they eat so much green-stuff, their eggs have the most wonderful deep yellow yolks. Cake sponges and ice creams made from their eggs always look much yellower than anything shop-bought! I take the risk with foxes (I've been lucky so far) because I know they are much happier when they are not marching up and down behind chicken wire all day looking for ways out.

During the winter months eggs are scarce and if you keep poultry you may have to buy some eggs – I had to buy only 12 eggs this winter. The chances are you may have a hen or two that moults early and begins laying again in January and one or two who go on laying into November before moulting. December is probably the worst month for eggs. If you have bred some new bantams/hens they may start laying in December if they were born in April/May.

Come the spring I am inundated with eggs and sell them or give them away to friends and neighbours. However I have three growing boys and there are many, many different ways I can use them in the kitchen. Eggs can be used almost exclusively for a main meal such as an omelette or for fried eggs to go with chips and beans for a quick meal, or for curried eggs for example. You can't be without them for cakes, custards, quiches, soufflés, meringues, ice creams, choux pastry, pancakes, as thickening agents for sauces, for binding meat balls, or for glazing pastry. That is why I have devoted the second section of this book to recipes giving you lots of ideas for using your eggs. Every recipe uses at least two eggs and most use three or more. I have also included recipes using just egg yolks and those using just egg whites which you may find useful.

Finally I would like to say my bantams live a full and happy life – some are already five or six years old. They are not laying like they were two or three years ago but it would be cruel to cull them now when we have enjoyed their eggs in the past. This book is not going to tell you, like many books, to kill off your flock after the second year of laying. This book is about keeping hens for pleasure and about encouraging others to keep hens in the hope of giving them a better life – a life that should be valued highly for where would we be without eggs?

SECTION ONE

1. ORIGINS OF THE HEN

Today's hen originated from the Red Jungle Fowl, Gallus Bankiva, which came from a wide area north of India stretching down through Burma and Malaya to Java. This bird can still be found living wild in the remote jungles of Burma and Java. The Red Jungle Fowl was originally a small bird that escaped its predator by flying up into the trees. It had long wings and a long tail. This bird would lay about 30 eggs a year in two clutches, one in the spring and one in late summer (this gives you an idea of how far the domestic fowl has progressed in its egg laying capacities!). When man started the domestication process these birds were developed for cock-fighting, an important sport for ancient civilizations and a favourite pastime of the Romans and the Greeks.

The first references to domestic fowl in literature occur in a Chinese encyclopaedia compiled in 1400BC. Chickens appear on Babylonian carvings dated at around 600BC. Later, around 400BC there are references in Plato in which he complains about people cock-fighting instead of labouring.

It is thought that fowl were introduced to Britain possibly by Phoenician sailors who had chickens transported to North Africa from India and brought them on to the Mediterranean coastal countries and then to Britain. Certainly the Romans found poultry already in Britain when they arrived in 54BC. Julius Caesar refers to the Britons as keeping fowl for amusement but not for eating, so we may assume cock-fighting was already prevalent.

The fowl that has remained the closest to the Red Jungle Fowl is the Old English Game which is very similar in appearance and was the breed developed over the centuries for cock-fighting. Cock-fighting became very popular in Britain between 1750 and 1849. Feeding and training the cocks was just as skilled a job as breeding them. They had to have their combs and wattles cut, their feathers and wings trimmed and their natural spurs were cut short so that artificial spurs or heels could be fitted. These could be anything up to three inches in length but two cocks fighting each other had to have spurs of equal length. They inflicted cleaner wounds than the natural spurs. Cocks also used their beaks and wings in the fights. A fight would carry on until one cock was killed or refused to continue fighting. In 1849 an Act was passed to make cock-fighting illegal in Britain but it is still practised in Spain, the Far East and some of the Latin-American countries.

It is thought that the Romans may have introduced the Dorking fowl to England when they settled here. The Dorking, characterised by its five toes, was described by Pliny and Columella in the first century. Possibly certain types of fowl were bred in different parts of the country but on the whole birds were still mainly bred for cock-fighting.

Bantam is the name of a town and district in the north west of Java. In 1595 the Dutch established themselves at Bantam and in 1602 the English occupied Java. The locals sold the beautiful jungle fowl from Bantam to the British who took them back to England. Eventually the word Bantam was used to describe all small poultry. Many breeds nowadays are available as large fowl or as miniatures which are commonly known as bantams but, technically, a true bantam does not have a large fowl counterpart.

Marco Polo on his journeys in the early 1300s described seeing chickens with 'fur' and must have been referring to the Silkie Breed, but it wasn't really until the 1800s that poultry, having been developed around the world, were imported into different countries and it was then that breeds of poultry began to be established in Britain. It is believed that Christopher Columbus brought the first chickens to America on his second trip there in 1493.

During the last 150 years the idea of keeping chickens for pleasure and not just for profit or recreation came into fashion with the start of Poultry Shows. Many smallholders were in evidence before the First World War and between the Wars many ex-servicemen set up poultry farms which were totally free-range. It was after the Second World War that more intensive systems began to be used such as deep litter, where hens were housed indoors on straw. Then in the Sixties and Seventies intensive battery operated systems were used extensively with hens spending their entire lives in small cages. Commercial egg production became big business – and it still is today. But over the last few years there have been campaigns against battery hens and there is definitely a move back to keeping hens in one's back garden for the benefit of free-range eggs (you know what your hens eat and therefore what has gone into the eggs) and because they make good family pets.

2. USEFUL FACTS

There are about 160 breeds of poultry. Modern hybrids are chickens that have been bred by crossing two breeds so that the production of the hybrid is greater than the parent stock – these include Black Rocks (Rhode Island Red x Barred Plymouth Rock), Speckledies (A Maran cross), Bovans Nera, White Star and Gold Line. There are also a number of autosexing breeds that have been developed in recent years. These have been bred so that the cockerels can be distinguished from the pullets by colour as soon as they are hatched (enabling breeders to cull the cockerels immediately). The first breed was Cambar, developed by crossing a Barred Plymouth Rock with a Gold Campine. Each new breed has the suffix –bar after it. In this way the Dorbar is a Dorking cross; Welbar (Welsummer cross) and the Legbar, which is perhaps the best known, can be gold, silver or cream and was developed by crossing the Leghorn with the Barred Plymouth Rock. The Cream Legbar, which is crested, was given a dose of Araucana blood so that it lays the unique turquoise eggs.

Breeds are divided into heavy or light and soft or hard-feathered. Light breeds are notorious for being non-sitters but good egg layers, rather than as table birds. They also have a tendency to be flighty. Examples of light breeds are Anconas, Leghorns and Welsummers. Heavy breeds are historically those developed for table or utility production (ie for commercial egg laying purposes). They have an excellent temperament so are also suitable as pets for children. Examples of heavy breeds are Marans, Orpingtons, Sussexes, Wyandottes, Plymouth Rocks and Rhode Island Reds. Hard-feathered breeds are the game varieties such as Old English Game and Modern Game whose origins lie, as previously mentioned, in cock-fighting. All other breeds are soft-feathered.

Breeds have arrived in Britain in the last couple of centuries from all over the world – Cochins and Pekins from China, Yokohamas from Japan, Malays from Asia, Leghorns and Anconas from Italy, Minorcas and Andalusians from Spain, Marans and Faverolles from France, Welsummers from Holland, Campines from Belgium, Rhode Island Reds, Wyandottes and Plymouth Rocks from America and Araucanas from Chile.

Most feather-legged hens go broody more readily than clean-legged hens and usually hens with white ear lobes lay white eggs. Bantams tend to be wilder and more flighty in temperament than large fowl.

Light Sussex Hen - an example of a soft-feathered heavy breed

Hens and bantams come in all sorts of colourings – different markings on the feathers help determine the colour.

Types of Feather Marking

Clockwise from top left: self, tipping, spangling, barring, striping, double lacing, single lacing, peppering, pencilling.

Combs can also vary between breeds.

Hens as Pets

There seem to be varied views on the life span of a hen. Some books state that it is possible for a hen to live up to 20 years of age. I would say that in practice hens and bantams are unlikely to live for more than 10 years and six to eight years is a more realistic expectation. The happier and more free-range the hens, the longer they are likely to live. Happy hens develop their own characters and bear little resemblance to those kept in battery cages or crowded conditions.

You should not consider that keeping chickens in your garden is going to be a profit-making business. You should do it more for the pleasure of keeping hens as pets and enjoying the supply of fresh, truly free-range eggs.

They can make excellent pets and children love collecting the eggs. If you decide to hatch some chicks, looking after them will give a child a great sense of responsibility and hopefully they will learn some interesting facts about reproduction. I think they make great pets because you get something back from them in the form of eggs – also they are not desperately time consuming and can look after themselves for the odd day and night as long as you make sure they have plenty of food and water. If you need to go away for a few days, neighbours can easily be persuaded to visit your hens and collect the eggs!

Getting your Hens

Firstly you don't need a cockerel in order for your hens to lay eggs, unlike wild birds who only lay an egg if it has been fertilised by a male. You may decide a cock will be unpopular with your neighbours. We had a cock which took to crowing at all hours, even at 2a.m. in the morning in the pitch black! You only need a cock if you want fertile eggs to breed from. When we bought our first four bantams, we chose two cross-bred pullets and two fully grown Light Sussex bantams. We called the two pullets Rosie and Goldie. However as Rosie grew, it became evident when she started crowing, that she was a cockerel and we called her Rockie. However she, now he, became so vicious that he would attack even my husband. In the end we took him back to his original owner and swapped him for a hen. It is best to get your hens at point-of-lay (POL) which will mean they are between 18 – 22 weeks and should start to lay soon after they settle down in their new home. If you go for a cross-breed or even a commercial or hybrid the birds should cost you between £5 and £10. Pure breeds tend to be more attractive and can cost anything between £10 and £40. You should look in your local newspaper or buy a copy of Poultry World, Farmers Guardian or Farmers Weekly (You may have to order these from your Newsagents). Country Smallholding is an excellent magazine and includes ads from breeders across the country with pure breeds for sale. You will also find chickens for sale at your local livestock market but these are best avoided as no one sends their best birds to market. Finally, before you go ahead, if you live in a built up area, you should ask the Environment Health Officer at the Council whether there are any by-laws to prevent you from keeping poultry.

Selling Eggs on a Small Scale

There is no requirement to register with the egg marketing inspectorate in order to sell surplus eggs to friends, neighbours, callers at the gate or at a market stall.

At one time you had to inform the local Environmental Health office if you wanted to sell your eggs but many local offices have apparently now waived this requirement.

3. HOUSING AND WHERE TO KEEP THEM

Having decided to keep hens or bantams, you need to think about their accommodation. You should have a secure hen house, preferably made of wood, which must be waterproof with perches and nest boxes. If you are a DIY enthusiast or know someone who is, you should be able to construct one. You need to make sure the roof is waterproof – roofing felt over a slatted wooden roof is a good option. The walls need to be weatherproof and the hen house does need to be well-ventilated because hens excrete half their daily amount while roosting/sleeping. If you decide to buy a hen house there are specialist catalogues featuring poultry houses which you can obtain. Particularly good examples are produced by Forsham Cottage Arks and the Domestic Fowl Trust.

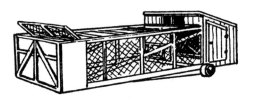

The Roller

Perches are essential for roosting and, where possible, should be 2 – 3ft (60 – 90cm) above the floor. Each laying bantam will require access to a nest box 12 – 15in (30 – 37cm) but larger birds will need 15 – 18in (37 – 45cm) of space. Once they have decided where to lay they will regularly queue up

15

for the spot and have, when desperate, been known to sit on top of each other in the same nest box! If possible, perches should be wooden slats, about 2½in (5cm) wide. Nest boxes should be placed in the darkest, cosiest corner of the hen house and filled with hay or straw. If you have several hens it is a good idea to have at least two nesting boxes.

You should by now have found out whether there are foxes in your area because this will affect what sort of housing you decide to use. At the same time you need to be thinking about how free-range your hens are going to be. You may want to keep them entirely enclosed, in which case Arks are a good option since they are usually on wheels and can be moved to fresh patches of grass. On the other hand you may want a hen house placed in an enclosed run or yard, in which case you need to think about fencing and whether you want to pay the extra expense to make it completely fox-proof. To give you a general idea, fox-proof fencing needs to be at least 6ft (2m) high with an overhang at the top to prevent the fox climbing over it, and needs to be dug into the ground to a depth of at least a foot (30cm) to prevent the fox digging under it. To be effective against foxes you need to buy chain link fencing as a determined fox will bite through ordinary chicken wire. A less expensive option would be to use black plastic fruit netting around your run and to lock your hens into a secure hen house each night. The netting should keep your hens in and away from your vegetable garden if that is your aim.

If you have a large garden and want your hens to be completely free-range you need only a secure hen house in which to close them up every evening and let them out every morning. If you grow vegetables, salads, etc., you should be warned that hens can very quickly ruin a vegetable patch. They particularly like spinach and all forms of lettuce – if you are going to give them the run of the garden you'll need to net susceptible vegetables. However, your hens can be a useful addition to the garden –

they are very good at breaking up the soil after you have dug over your vegetable garden in the winter; they forage for pests and produce droppings, which are one of the best fertilisers you can get. My bantams love following me around when I am digging the vegetable garden and are practically under my fork as I turn the soil and they grab the worms.

If you want to prevent your hens flying out of a run then you may want to clip their wings. You need to cut back the primary feathers on one wing only so that the hen will be unbalanced and unable to fly. You must not cut too near the quills as this may make her bleed. As a general rule you need to clip the first three or four flight feathers back to half length. On heavy breeds this should prevent them getting more than a few inches off the ground but the lighter breeds will still be able to fly up to 6ft (2m) even with one wing clipped.

Electric fencing is a possibility to keep your hens enclosed and the advantage to this is you can move the fencing to new patches of grass. Obviously this is not a good idea if you have young children.

You may have heard about different systems used for keeping chickens. They are:

The **Fold or Ark System** (a house complete with its own covered run) which is moved onto fresh grass every few days.

The **Deep Litter System** (an intensive system) in which hens are not let out at all but are housed in one big building on straw which builds up and is usually removed once a year. Artificial lighting would be used in this system, thus ensuring a good level of egg production.

The **Straw Yard System** which is similar to a deep litter system but the hens are confined in a straw covered yard with access to a hen house.

Permanent (Dirt) Run is a commonly used way of keeping hens with a hen house and a permanent run, which begins as grass but very soon becomes mud in winter and dry earth in summer. If the system can incorporate two runs, which can be rested alternately, this will give your hens more access to green-stuff.

The two extremes to these systems which have already been mentioned are the **Battery System** and the **Free-range System,** which is naturally the best arrangement for all concerned.

The Dangers of Foxes, Badgers, Dogs and Cats

Foxes are the most common and dangerous killers of hens and usually strike first thing in the morning or at dusk, although in urban areas foxes seem to be seen more and more wandering around during the day. One often hears stories of foxes killing all the hens a family owns in one go. People wonder why a fox has to kill every hen in sight and only carry off one or two. He only does this because he has been disturbed: left to his own devices he would come back and carry off each carcass to bury as food for the future. He is an opportunist and cleverer than we suppose. Badgers also kill hens but do so strictly at night.

Rats can very easily kill a brood of chicks, as can crows, magpies, stoats or weasels.

Dogs have attacked and killed my bantams in the past and we had a cat who would come during the day and steal chicks. If a dog kills any of your hens you can claim damages against the dog's owner (provided you know whose dog it is) under the Animals Act 1971 – *An Act to make provision with respect to civil liability for damage done by animals and with respect to the protection of livestock from dogs; and for purposes connected with those matters.* This Act replaces the Dogs (Amendment) Act 1928 (injury to cattle or poultry).

4. FEEDING

A normal sized hen needs about 100g, 4oz of food a day in the form of grain. This can be supplied as mixed poultry grain, layers pellets or layers mash. Mixed grain consists of wheat, barley, oats and maize. For pellets and mash these grains are ground down. Pellets are small and cylindrical – they are clean and easy for hens to eat but if confined the hens can get bored. Mash on the other hand keeps the birds busy for hours and can be fed dry or wet. For chicks the grains are ground down to form crumbs. Chick crumbs also contain a coccidiostat as an aid in the prevention of a disease known as coccidiosis.

If your hens are confined, there is a danger in them overfeeding on layers mash or pellets and this danger applies especially to pullets who may start laying too early and prolapse may occur (see prolapse on page 32). It is advisable to start pullets on a low protein diet of wheat to avoid early maturity.

Since my bantams are free-range they forage during the day, eating insects (slugs, I hope), plenty of worms, grass and other green-stuff. I feed them on left-over pasta (which they love), rice, bread, bits of pastry, cooked potatoes and other vegetables and lettuce leaves. Most hens also enjoy bananas and fruit with pips, tomatoes, sunflower seeds, and bits of hard cheese. Kitchen scraps to avoid are anything salty, citrus peel, banana skins, uncooked potato peelings, chocolate and fish bones.

I buy mixed poultry grain from a local feed merchant – this contains maize which always disappears first from the feed containers. It is the maize, which along with grass, produces the yellow pigment found in egg yolks. I leave it to my bantams to balance their own diets by taking what they want from the food hoppers and from eating wild food. This seems to work perfectly well.

Hens producing eggs on a regular basis also need calcium in their diet. If you live on chalky soil they may be able to pick up enough from the soil, as mine do. But if you notice the shells on their eggs are particularly thin you may have to supplement their diet with extra calcium. You will need to buy crushed oyster or cockle shells from your local feed merchant, or you could use your own egg shells but you should bake them first and then crush them, to avoid your hens getting a taste for fresh egg shells (which might lead to egg eating). They also need grit, which helps them digest food in their crop, and they pick this up from the soil. If confined, you will need to buy grit and provide this for them. Hens and bantams also need fresh water at all times. A clove of garlic in the drinking water is said to be a good tonic for hens.

Special drinking containers can be bought from suppliers, as can automatic feeders which release more grain from an inner container as the hens eat it. It is advisable to keep your grain in dustbins with lids to deter vermin such as rats and mice.

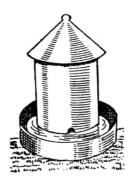

It is certainly true that the more access your hens have to grass and green-stuff the darker yellow the egg yolks. If your hens are confined without access to grass, then they need as much green-stuff as possible. It is a good idea to hang a cabbage or other green vegetable up by a length of cord so that it is off the ground. Hens can then pick at it more easily than if left on the ground. Nettles are also a good source of minerals and you can give your hens fresh or dried grass clippings.

Digestive System

Chickens do not have teeth so that anything they eat goes down their throat whole and into the crop. The crop acts as a storehouse for the gizzard, which is a sort of bag in the digestive system. When the gizzard is empty, food will move down from the crop and small amounts of grit in the gizzard will help to grind the food.

Hen Manure

The droppings are a very useful bonus to keeping hens. Lawns on which hens are allowed to roam receive excellent conditioning and end up much greener and lusher as a result. However, if your children also like to play on the lawn they may object to the amount of 'chicken pooh' they get on their shoes, clothes and hands!

Poultry manure provides an excellent fertiliser for your vegetable garden. It is richer than horse manure and consists of nitrogen, phosphates (phosphorus) and potash. It contains semi-solid urine (hens do not urinate separately) which is the white part of the droppings and is the nitrogen element. The manure makes an excellent compost activator. For your compost heap to work it needs a great increase of bacteria in a short time and nitrogen and phosphorus are needed for this –

chicken manure is the answer, so collect it up and add to your compost bin. The best thing is to layer it with the other things you are adding.

Alternatively you can collect chicken droppings straightaway from under the perches, sprinkle with superphosphates which will help dry them (and increases the phosphorus) and dig it into your vegetable patch. If you use it immediately, maximum advantage will be gained from the plant nutrients (phosphates, potash and nitrogen) and vegetables that will benefit include tomatoes, courgettes, radishes, spinach and cabbage and beans. Poultry manure is also an excellent fertiliser for black- and redcurrant bushes and raspberries, although it should not be used for apple and pear trees. Do not, however, use the manure fresh in your flower garden as it will be too strong and may scorch your plants. If poultry droppings are left in the open and get wet, the nitrogen gets washed away and they lose their valuable nutrients. If you have the time and are keen to store your poultry manure, a good mixture would be poultry droppings, half the amount in earth and in superphosphates and a quarter of wood ash.

Your hens' feathers can be useful too. If you bury some feathers around your blackcurrant bushes these provide slow-release nitrogen, which is just what blackcurrants need to stimulate new growth after you have pruned them each year.

5. CHARACTERISTICS, BEHAVIOUR AND HABITS

A special characteristic of poultry is that they have vibration sensitive organs. These are distributed all over their skin but in greatest concentration on the legs and they will pick up any vibrations from the ground or in the air. This means that the approach of an enemy is detected very quickly. Since our domestic fowl have developed from wild chickens living in forests where their vision was limited by trees and undergrowth, their eyes are focused for small objects up to five metres away but only for larger objects about 50 metres away. Consequently they are not happy to move more than 50 metres from their housing, which they like to keep in sight. To see things in three dimensions, chickens need to fix objects first with the left eye and then with the right. This is why you see their heads moving from side to side and they walk in a zigzag fashion. Their sense of colour is well developed and their hearing is very good. Chickens have no outer ears but a short auditory canal is protected by feathers and a flap of skin. They can produce a great variety of sounds, many more than most other types of birds. Chicks for example begin cheeping while still in their eggs. Once born, they can recognise the voice of their mother up to 15 metres away and likewise Mother Hen can recognise her chicks cheeping. She calls her chicks to give them food using a short, deep tone. But when she calls them to crawl under her for sleep, she uses a long deep tone broken up by high-pitched ones. Fully grown cockerels, of course, crow and this is mainly as a sign of their power but also for the joy of it. Hens cluck gently to themselves as a sign of well-being but use a different sound when alarmed by something. Hens make a different sound again when they proudly announce that they have laid an egg rather like a cock with his crowing.

A Typical Day

A day in the life of a chicken runs something like this:

In the summer when there is plenty of light, a hen's day will start at sunrise with feeding and probably egg laying. There follows a period during which hens will preen their feathers and clean the more inaccessible parts of their bodies with their beaks. The feathers are also oiled by the beak. Oil is picked up from the preen gland on the tail and distributed on the feathers. My bantams tend to do this standing on top of their various hutches, especially in winter when the grass is wet. At about midday hens often like to relax in a dust-bath and doze in a cool place if it is hot or in the sunshine (a form of sun-bathing!) – they lie on one side and spread out their uppermost wing – they look quite strange but don't be alarmed – it is quite normal. Later on, a second peak of activity occurs in which the cock may be mating with his hens and, if not confined, all your hens will be out and about foraging for interesting food. They will also want to fill up their crops ready for the night. Hens like to sleep in groups on a perch in their houses or, like some of mine, roost up in a tree for the night. Pecking order is evident at this time because the hens who come first in the pecking order will want to sleep on the highest perches. Once they are settled on their perches, hens will retract their necks, shut their eyes, put their heads under a wing and go to sleep.

The Pecking Order

The order of power is firmly established by the pecking order.

If you have a group of hens with a cock then he will be at the top of the pecking order. Hens under him will fight to be the second most powerful by pecking each other. If a hen loses a fight she will adopt a subservient pose, with her body lowered and legs bent. Incidentally, the larger a hen's comb is, the more she will be feared by others and she will probably automatically gain second place in the pecking order. If there is no cockerel in the group, the hen with the largest comb will probably be boss and will take on a male role – she may even crow! New hens introduced to an established group may take a while to achieve a pecking order – on the whole older hens will be more self-confident and expect a high rank while younger, more timid hens may go straight to the bottom of the pecking order. If you have two cocks, one will become dominant, or you may find they fight, especially if they are enclosed and you may have to separate them. If you introduce new hens to an established flock you should isolate them for the first few days to avoid bullying problems. It must also be said here that often hens and bantams develop friendships just like humans - sometimes two or three hens will stick together during the day and at night.

Mating

Cocks usually do most of their mating between April and October. A cock will approach a hen and stand erect in front of her with his neck feathers ruffled. He will then dance around her with the wing nearest her spread downwards. The hen, if a submissive one, will duck down and allow him to mount her. He will use his wings to maintain his balance and grip her by the nape of her neck while he mates. The cock may also be quite cunning, luring his hens over by calling them to food and then jumping on them! The problems with mating occur with the high-ranking hens who will often object to mating by flying off and refusing to let the cock near them. We had one bantam hen called Georgie who was horribly persecuted by a cock. He was always chasing her and she would fly up on to a pergola attached to our house to avoid him – needless to say we had to get rid of him to give her some peace.

Dust Baths

If your hens are confined, it is important that you make up a dust bath for them. Use a large box and half fill it with dry earth, sand or ashes. Hens like to squat down and shake themselves with movements of the body and wings so that their feathers get covered in dust. The dust trickles through their feathers and onto their skin. In this way they clean themselves and the dust helps remove many of the parasites such as lice which infest the skin. Once finished, hens will give their feathers a good shake and probably go back to searching for food.

Moulting

The natural moulting time is late summer or early autumn. Most hens will stop laying then and cocks will stop mating. Occasionally a hen will go on laying while moulting and a few may resume laying while moulting is still in progress. Moulting usually lasts between eight and 12 weeks. Feathers are lost from the head, neck, breast and body and lastly from the wings and tail. Hens born in the spring and summer will not usually moult until the autumn of the next year. Usually it is the poor egg layers that moult early and the better the layer, the later in the year she will moult.

6. EGG LAYING

Chicks born in early spring, known as pullets until they are a year old, will start to lay, with luck, in November and certainly before Christmas. Chicks that are born later in June or July will probably not start laying until January or February. Eggs from a newly-laying pullet will be small in comparison to the size that she will lay when fully grown.

An easy pointer to a hen that is laying is a red comb which is warm to the touch. On a more technical basis, your can pick her up and feel for her pelvic bones which should be about 5 cm (2in) or the width of three fingers apart. You can also test the distance between the end of the breastbone and the pelvic bones – if she is laying, there should be a width of four fingers. When she stops laying, her comb will be pale and the vent (the opening between the pelvic bones) will close to one finger's width.

Beak pigment in certain breeds can also help tell you if a hen is laying. Breeds such as Leghorns, Wyandottes and Rhode Island Reds have yellow pigment in their skin, legs and beak called xanthophylls. At the beginning of the laying period this pigment will be seen in the beak and legs. As the hen begins to lay, the pigment which is obtained from such food as yellow maize and green plants will now be required for the yolks. The pigment in the beak which starts at the base, when she is not laying will move up the beak and will be seen as a ring of pigment in the middle of her beak when she is laying. It will then reach the tip of her beak and will gradually fade away as she continues to lay. When the pigment reappears at the base of the beak this means she has stopped laying.

The yolk of the egg is formed in the ovary and is then released to travel down the oviduct. In the longest part of the oviduct much of the albumen is added and also the cord-like chalazae which keep the yolk in place. The egg is driven down by peristaltic squeezing movements to the isthmus where it receives the shell membrane. It then moves to the uterus (shell gland) where it stays for about 20 hours while the shell-forming glands get to work. More albumen is added here and calcium is released as the main constituent of the shell. The shape and colour of the shell are also determined in the uterus. Finally the bloom or cuticle is added and the egg is laid. In all, the egg has taken about 25 hours to form from ovulation to laying.

Female reproductive system

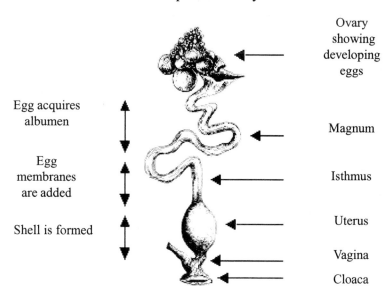

Ovary showing developing eggs

Egg acquires albumen

Magnum

Egg membranes are added

Isthmus

Shell is formed

Uterus

Vagina

Cloaca

The hen will stand to lay her egg – it is quite fascinating to watch this process if you happen to be there at the right time. In a regularly laying bird, an egg is laid about every 26 hours.

So within an hour of one egg being laid the process starts again. In winter the time between eggs increases so eggs are laid about every 27 to 28 hours. A hen will, in a natural state, lay 20 or so eggs – this is called a 'clutch' – and then she will have a 'pause' lasting several days and if she doesn't go broody will start laying another clutch of eggs. Hens usually have some time off laying while they are moulting in winter and will start laying again in January or February but probably only lay about half what they manage to lay at their peak in April or May, as the days lengthen. In August and September, hens will reduce the amount of eggs they are laying as the days shorten and then stop completely when they come in to moult.

Light plays a vital role in egg production. It affects a small organ behind the eye which in turn sends messages to the ovary and affects the ovulation process. So it is natural for a hen to lay in the spring and go out of lay in the shorter days of autumn. Professional eggs farmers overcome this problem by using artificial light and are therefore able to maintain the same amount of light every day which evens out the egg production.

You may find that your pullets or indeed two or three-year-old hens are reluctant to start laying in February. This is when you can start using layers mash or pellets. It is best to feed layers mash in the morning and grain in the afternoon, otherwise they gorge themselves in the morning on grain which is full of starch and only become fat.

Problems with Eggs

Strange Eggs

Occasionally your hen may lay a **tiny egg** which has no yolk. The egg may contain a fragment of tissue torn away from the ovary and as it passes down the oviduct it serves as a nucleus which stimulates the internal mechanism to operate and produce a tiny egg - it is known as a cock or witch egg. This problem normally occurs in new pullets or in hens at the end of their laying season.

Double-yolked eggs are sometimes produced by pullets in their first laying season. This is caused by two eggs separating from the ovary at the same time and joining into one egg.

Soft-shelled eggs are eggs with no shell, just the membrane around the egg. This may happen in young pullets - the egg goes down through the oviduct so quickly that there is no time for the shell to be made. Sometimes the pullets are adjusting to metabolism and the first few eggs will have no shell, but after a couple of weeks the eggs should be normal. If the egg has a very thin shell, your hen may not be getting enough calcium or Vitamin D in her diet and you could try giving her crushed oyster shells and some cod liver oil in her feed. If your hen is still laying soft-shelled eggs after two or three weeks, it may be due to some inherent weakness in the strain which does not allow proper assimilation of calcium, or an inherent malfunctioning of the reproductive tract; in this case unfortunately you may have to cull her. Shell-less eggs in the nest box on a regular basis would inevitably lead to the vice of **egg-eating.** Once hens start eating eggs it can become a habit difficult to cure. One remedy would be to make the nest boxes as dark as possible and to collect your eggs more frequently.

Prolapse

This may occur as a result of straining to lay too large an egg or because a pullet starts laying eggs before its body is ready. The hen's bottom will look lower than usual because the vent muscles are pushed out. You will see a red mass of tissue pushing out through the vent. You can bathe the area or apply some Vaseline and gently but firmly press it back with a warm piece of flannel.

Egg Bound

If your hen seems to be constantly going to the nest box but laying no eggs and shows signs of distress, it may be assumed that she is egg bound. The egg may be too large and will have got stuck, even though it is ready to be laid. You could try holding the bottom half of your afflicted hen over steaming water for several minutes. But do not hold her too close to the steam and make sure she is calm. This treatment generally relaxes and softens that part of the body, and the egg should be released. If the egg breaks inside the hen it will probably kill her but she will also die if she cannot pass the egg. You could also try the old fashioned cure of pouring a spoonful of olive oil down your hen's throat. I have not had this problem so have tried neither remedy myself.

Egg Peritonitis (internal laying)

Egg yolks drop into the body cavity, instead of entering the oviduct and death usually occurs within 24 hours.

Blood or Meat Spots and Rings

You may see a small blood spot or ring at the edge of the yolk or a meat spot in the white when you break one of your hens' eggs. These are completely harmless. They are caused by the rupture of a blood vessel in the ovary which may have occurred due to a sudden fright.

Our Domestic Fowl Trust Penthouse

Our bantam,
Tilly and her
brood of chicks

A Silkie - Sharon Jackson, Foxfield Fowls, Ringwood

A Millefleur Barbu d'Uccle Bantam - Sharon Jackson, Foxfield
Fowls, Ringwood

A Welsummer hen and cock - Susie Wilson, Hilcott, Wiltshire

A black Pekin hen and cock - Susie Wilson, Hilcott, Wiltshire

Our one and only Old English Game hen given to us by a friend

Two of our silver-laced Wyandotte hens

One of our Araucana cross breeds, layers of blue eggs

A Frizzle bantam - Clair Housden, Saffron Walden

A trio of gold Silkies - Clair Housden, Saffron Walden

Red mottled Leghorns and a Scots Grey - Clair Housden

Sebrights - Clair Housden, Saffron Walden

Red mottled
Leghorn cock
- Clair Housden,
Saffron Walden

Our Araucana crosses taking a drink from a drinking
fountain bought from the Domestic Fowl Trust

Dogs can be trained to be good with bantams!

Some bantams will make a nest anywhere!

Time for a spot of sunbathing!

7. BROODY HENS AND HATCHING CHICKS

To Stop your Hen being Broody

Your hens may become broody two or three times in the spring and summer or even autumn. To stop your hen being broody, put her in an airy coop with a slatted or wire mesh floor where there is no opportunity for nesting. Ideally after a few days isolated in a coop she will give up feeling broody and, if you then feed her on layers pellets, she should start laying again quite quickly.

Broody Hens

Firstly, if you have one of the non-sitting breeds such as Welsummer, Ancona, Leghorn or Hamburgh, your hens shouldn't go broody at all. Other hens will generally go broody after they have laid between 12 and 20 eggs if you leave these eggs in their nests. Obviously, if you collect the eggs every day, they will not go broody as easily. If you are allowing your hen to go broody on eggs she has laid in her own nest, she will automatically make her own storage conditions. Each day she will move or turn her eggs. A small amount of grease from her body is transferred on to the eggs and this helps prevent the loss of moisture during storage. She also warms the eggs every time she sits to lay an egg and sits longer as the time for broodiness approaches. You can use a pullet as a broody but you should make sure that she has been laying for at least two months before you allow her to sit.

The Nest

If you have a chance to prepare a nest for your broody hen, you should use a small box with a wire mesh floor to prevent rats burrowing their way into the nest. Place a turf with the grass uppermost in the box. If you turn the turf over and hollow out some of the earth this will create a dip. It is important that the nest is on turf as this allows natural moisture to come up from the earth. If the weather is very dry while your hen is sitting, you can pour some warm water on the outer rim of the turf to keep it moist. Using hay or straw, make the nest circular with a slight dip in the middle. Don't make the nest too hollow or eggs will roll together and crack, or too shallow so that the eggs roll out. The nest box should have some sort of ventilation and should be part of a coop or attached to a wire run, or at least enclosed in a yard to prevent intruders gaining access.

Sitting on the Eggs

If you don't have a cockerel but want to hatch some chicks, you can buy in fertile or hatching eggs from poultry keepers or from the Domestic Fowl Trust to put under a broody hen. First make sure she is definitely broody and has been sitting, after you have moved her to your prepared nest, either on crock eggs or some of your eggs for two or three days. Other indications that she is broody will be that she looks all puffed up, clucks continuously and doesn't like you interfering with her or her eggs – she may peck you. If you check her in the evening and she is still sitting, this is a good indication that she is broody. You should delouse your broody hen with louse powder at this point as you don't want her disturbed by fleas as she sits. No one can of course guarantee the fertility of the eggs so use more eggs than the number of chicks that you want so as not to be disappointed. You should put an odd number of eggs underneath her as these make a circle. About nine eggs is enough for a small bantam, but a larger hen can sit on up to 15 eggs. It is important to allow any eggs that you have ordered to rest for 12 hours after transportation. Eggs can be stored for up to 10 days before starting incubation. If you are using your own eggs, make sure they are an average size and good shape. If you are storing fertile eggs until you have enough to set under the hen together, they should not be too hot, as embryonic development will start at 20°C (68°F) or above, or too cold. An optimum temperature is around 13°C (55°F). You should store them pointed end down or on their side and you should turn them once a day; this is to stop the embryo from floating upwards and adhering to the shell membrane. Do not wash the eggs unless they are dirty, in which case you should use warm water. Place the eggs under your broody hen in the evening when she is calm.

Once a day your hen will need to leave her nest to eat, drink, defecate and take a dust bath. She should not be off the eggs for more than about 20 minutes. The eggs will cool off during this time but this is important for their development as it allows fresh air into the eggs. If she is reluctant to leave her nest each day you should gently pick her up, taking care that no eggs are concealed between her wings or feathers, and take her to where you have placed food and water. It is a good idea to check the eggs when your broody hen comes off the nest and if any have broken you must remove them. Also you should wash any eggs that have become stained in warm water before returning them to a clean nest of straw. Check that her feet are clean when she goes back on her nest.

You should feed your hen a diet of mixed poultry corn while she is sitting. Layers pellets are unsuitable as they pass through her digestive system too quickly and cause her to defecate on the eggs. The maize in the mixed grain is particularly important as it is full of protein.

If at any time your broody decides to desert her eggs and cannot be persuaded back to her nest you may be able to save the eggs. Eggs that have become cold can be immersed in water heated to 105°F and then given to another sitting hen.

Your broody hen will turn her eggs several times a day with her beak. The moist warmth from her body moistens the surface of the eggs. Also, if she is sitting on earth, this helps to produce humidity. Moisture, heat and oxygen are the essential conditions for successful hatching. When a hen is broody the normal warmth of her body is increased by the condition of the blood-vessels in that part of her body coming into contact with the eggs. These become distended and the accelerated blood flow causes the temperature of the atmosphere around the eggs to rise to about 103°F. The germ is at the upper surface of the egg and when the hen returns to her nest after her short break she will shuffle and rearrange her eggs, turning them as she does so. If the eggs were not turned there would be danger of the germ sticking to the shell membrane, which would result in the death of the embryo. The turning also helps to diffuse the oxygen which is conducted through the albumen to the germ.

Candling Eggs

This was originally done by holding the egg up to the light of a candle to check on embryo growth. Nowadays you can buy a candler which has a light bulb attached. This is basically a concentrated source of light so that you can see through the shell and check the development of the chick. This can be done on the sixth or seventh day and on the seventeenth day and allows you to discard eggs where the embryo has not developed. On the seventh day, if the egg is fertile, you will see a dark shadow with veins running through it – it looks something like a spider with red legs. An infertile egg is clear and shows the light clearly through it. On the seventeenth day fertile eggs will show a dense black mass with a clearly defined air cell in the broad end.

Hatching

Bantam eggs usually hatch before those of a hen, taking between 18 to 20 days rather that the 21 days for a hen. The chick will start cheeping while still inside its egg and this will trigger the hen's maternal instincts. Shortly before hatching, the chicks take in the yolk sac via the umbilical cord which then closes up. The chick will then raise its head and the egg-tooth on top of the beak will press a hole in the shell, causing the egg to crack open and the chick to hatch.

If you have bought day-old-chicks which you want your broody to foster, you need to introduce them during the first night after *her* eggs have hatched, otherwise she will not accept them. Her maternal instinct is very strong and the first day is rather like a photograph – she has good colour vision and will accept various different coloured chicks but only on that first day. She cannot count but that photograph of her chicks will be imprinted on her brain and if you try and add a new chick on the third day she will not accept it and may even kill it. It is not a good idea to mix bantam and large fowl chicks due to the difference in size and the obvious risk of bullying.

If eggs under your broody still remain unhatched after 21 days you can test them by placing them in a bowl of hand hot water. Those that sink then bob about after a few seconds contain live chicks and should be put back under your hen. If after a couple of minutes there is no sign of life they should be discarded. You can also shake the eggs and if you can detect liquid inside you will know these have not developed either.

There is a lot of information here about what you should and shouldn't do for your broody hen and her nest. If your hens are totally free-range, they may not need any help in producing a brood of chicks. My Buff Sussex Bantam disappeared last year and re-appeared three weeks later with five beautiful black chicks in tow (she had mated with an Araucana cock). We never found out where her nest had been but she obviously organised herself very well and didn't need any human interference.

Feeding and Rearing the Chicks

Chicks do not need anything to eat for at least the first 24 hours because the yolk in their stomachs gives them all the nourishment they need during this period. While her chicks are hatching, Mother Hen will sit for approximately 48 hours and manage without food or water. You should try and leave her alone for this period.

Then start your chicks on chick crumbs, which they need to eat for the first six to eight weeks. You can also give them breadcrumbs mixed with chopped up boiled eggs. Mother Hen will be happy to eat the chick feed as she gradually regains her strength after days of semi-starvation. Newly born chicks should be fed every couple of hours. Drinking water is also very important.

Some people like to use a specially designed rearing coop in which the hen stays behind bars and cannot disturb the chicks as they feed, drink and run about. Your broody hen might become quite agitated once she is up and about, scratching the feed all over the place, upsetting the water and scattering her chicks in the process. It is therefore best not to put hay or straw in the coop once the chicks have hatched, as Mother Hen will scratch that up too and may inadvertently kick her chicks and kill or injure them.

If you do not have a rearing coop, a simple, small hen house with run attached will be ideal. In any case, if you are moving

your brood to new quarters, leave this until the evening about 24 hours after they have all hatched.

After about five weeks the chicks will have grown enough feathers not to need to sleep under Mother Hen any more. At around eight weeks the broody hen will slowly lose her attachment to her chicks and return to the flock. She may at this time turn suddenly against the male chicks in particular, and start pecking them. Her maternal instincts disappear and her hormones are now geared for egg laying and she may start laying eggs almost straightaway. The brood of chicks however will tend to stick together once their Mum leaves.

Meanwhile, your chicks will not become sexually mature until 21 weeks. They then may start laying eggs but everything depends on the time of the year that they hatched. If the days are shortening when they reach sexual maturity then they may not start laying until early spring. If they have been born in February for example then they may start laying in July.

Hatching Eggs in an Incubator

You may wish to use an incubator to hatch your chicks. These vary in price and quality enormously and you need to follow the manufacturers' instructions very carefully. You will either have stored fertile eggs from one of your hens, or you may have bought hatching eggs. All the eggs need to be put in the incubator at the same time and they usually take slightly longer than the 21 days to hatch. The advantage of using an incubator is that you can hatch new chicks at any time of the year and you don't need to use a hen who would otherwise be laying eggs. When all the chicks have hatched you need to move them to a brooder. As a general rule you will need to keep the chicks in the brooder for five or six weeks; then you can turn off the heat and keep them inside for another two weeks before transferring them outside at eight weeks, at which time you can also start feeding adult rations.

Getting Rid of Surplus Cockerels

Your main problem when rearing chicks is going to be getting rid of the cockerels. You only really need one cock to 25 hens and since you get an average of 60% male chicks when you hatch a brood, you are almost certain to have to dispose of some of your cockerels. If you are very lucky you may be able to give them away. If you have a pure bred cockerel you may find a breeder who needs one. Otherwise they must be killed. But do make sure there are no small children around when this is done. The old fashioned way is to wring their necks but this is no job for an amateur. A trip to an obliging vet may be the best option.

8. BREEDS

ANCONA

The Ancona hen, as the name suggests, originated in Italy. Both the cock and hen are similar in colour – a mottled black and white. The single comb on the female tends to flop over on one side. The hens lay white eggs and are very similar to Leghorns.

ANDALUSIAN

This breed owes its name to the province of Andalusia in Spain and is one of the oldest Mediterranean breeds. The Andalusian is blue, probably developed from crossing black and white stock. The female has a distinctive comb which flops to one side of its head. It has white ear lobes and lays white eggs.

ARAUCANA

Araucanas were bred by the Indians from the Arauca Province of Northern Chile, South America, who refused to let the Spanish conquerors crossbreed their hens. They are the only hens in the world to lay turquoise eggs (colours vary between green, olive and blue) but no one knows quite why they do. Araucanas are crested and have faces covered with thick muffling. They come in many colours including lavender, blue, silver, black and white. There is also a Rumpless variation of the breed which, as the name suggests, does not have a tail but is favoured because it lays a large egg in relation to its body size.

AUSTRALORP

The Australorp is an abbreviation for Australian Black Orpington and is the prototype of the Black Orpington. It is a stocky breed with a single comb and black legs.

BARNEVELDER

This breed originated in Holland named after the district, Barneveld. Barnevelders were imported into Britain in the early 1900s. The hens lay deep brown eggs. Colour variations are black, double laced (black with beetle green sheen), partridge and silver. This is a heavy soft-feathered breed and the bantams are replicas of their large fowl counterparts.

BELGIAN BEARDED BANTAMS

Three varieties are standardised in Britain: **BARBU D'UCCLE** (Bearded Uccle) is, as the name suggests, heavily feathered around the neck with feathered feet. It has a single comb and comes in many colour variations including black mottled, lavender, porcelaine, millefleur and laced-blue. The amazing choice of colours in these bantams is probably unrivalled in any other breed. They lay small cream eggs. **BARBU D'ANVERS** (Bearded Antwerp) differs from the Barbu d'Uccle in that it has clean legs, a rose comb and in the males the wings are carried very low, almost vertically. **BARBU DE WATERMAEL** (Bearded Watermael) is crested and clean-legged, small and perky. All three remind one of a human wearing an overcoat with the collar turned up.

BRAHMA

The Brahma is a very old breed supposedly from India and

early pictures show that it was very similar to the Cochin from China. The name Brahma is taken from the river Brahmaputra in India. However, it is now generally agreed that the Brahma was created in America from Shanghais or Cochins imported from China in the 1800s and crossed with Grey Chittagongs (Malay type birds from India). It is known that a crate of Brahmas was sent to Queen Victoria in 1852 and thus the breed was introduced to Britain. Brahmas have distinctive feathered legs and feet and a pea comb. They come in a variety of types and colours including dark, gold, light, birchen and dark columbian. They are a heavy, soft-feathered breed and lay tinted eggs.

CAMPINE

The Campine is an ancient breed from Belgium which has a very attractive barring or pencilling on the feathers, although the neck is without markings. Bred in silver or gold, the Campine was used to produce Pencilled Hamburghs. More recently it has been used in the production of the first Autosexing breed, the Cambar.

COCHIN

The Cochin originally came in the 1850s from China where it was known as the Shanghai. It originally had clean legs and became very popular in this country owing to its size and laying powers. However exhibition breeders turned the Cochin into a 'bag of feathers' and it eventually lost its good name. Now similar to the Brahma with feathered legs and feet, it is a heavy soft-feathered breed and lays tinted eggs. There are no miniature versions of this bird.

CROAD LANGSHAN

Langshans were first imported into Britain by Major Croad from China where they are said to have originated in the Monasteries. Most common in black with a beautiful green tinge, there is also a rare white variety. They both have a single comb and lightly feathered legs and feet. Langshans lay deep brown eggs. There is also a Modern Langshan breed which has been developed along different lines.

DERBYSHIRE REDCAP

The Derbyshire Redcap originated in Britain, and is a sturdy breed, though sometimes classified as a light soft-feathered type. It lays white eggs and has a distinctive large rose comb. Redcaps are brown in colour with feathers tipped in black.

DORKING

It is thought that the Dorking is one of the oldest domesticated fowl, possibly introduced into Britain by the Romans, and was described by Pliny in his Natural History. The five toes are a distinctive feature of the Dorking. It is a heavy, soft-feathered breed laying tinted eggs. In the female, the single comb flops over to one side. This breed is on the Rare Breeds Survival Trust list. However the breed has been used in autosexing to produce the Dorbar.

DUTCH BANTAM

The Dutch Bantam originated in Holland but wasn't introduced to Britain until the Sixties. Available in a multitude of colours, they are popular both as pets and exhibition birds. The Dutch Bantam is an alert, active bird with an upright jaunty appearance. Wings are carried low and although ear lobes are white, they lay tinted eggs.

FAVEROLLE

This breed originated in the village of Faverolles in Northern France and Dorking, Houdan and Cochin were all used to develop it. It was imported into Britain in the late 1800s. A breed that combines a beard, muffs and a single comb with feathered legs, it is also unusual in that it has five toes on each foot like the Dorking. It comes in a variety of interesting colours including laced-blue, cuckoo, ermine, salmon and white. The Faverolle is a heavy soft-feathered breed which lays tinted eggs.

FRIZZLE

This is a breed which has feathers more or less completely curved the wrong way. The Frizzle is an old heavy soft-feathered breed thought to have been widespread originally in parts of the Far East such as Sumatra, Java and the Philippines. Available in a variety of colours such as buff, white or columbian, the Frizzle is more popular as a bantam than a large fowl and lays white or tinted eggs.

HAMBURGH

Hamburghs are rose-combed with white ear lobes, slate legs and long bodies. They are a light, soft-feathered breed which come in very attractive colours – gold, silver or black. The gold and silver can be pencilled (with pencilling straight across in fine parallel lines of rich green-black) or spangled (black tip to the feather). The bantams are miniature versions of the large fowl but have not been bred in black.

INDIAN GAME

A heavy breed, the Indian or Cornish Game originated in Cornwall and is rumoured to have been brought to Britain by the Phoenicians before the Romans arrived. They are very poor egg layers but were popular for meat in the past. Indian Game are a strange shape with a very thick body, wide breast and broad shoulders. There are various different types of bird, namely the Indian, Dark Indian, Jubilee and blue-laced Indian Game. Bantams are also available.

JAPANESE BANTAM

These are true bantams from Japan and come in three types of feathering – silkie, frizzle or normal and in various colours, but most commonly black-tailed white or mottled. They are very squat with the shortest legs of any breed and their shanks and thighs are developed in such a way that it is sometimes difficult to tell whether a bantam is sitting or standing. Japanese Bantams have a long upright tail with their wings carried low.

LEGHORN

A very popular light breed which originated from the Port of Leghorn in Italy and was imported into Britain in the late 1800s, with white first and then brown Leghorns. Leghorns have had the longest life of any of the productive breeds ever introduced. It was a light bird originally, and from old pictures it would seem that this type of bird with a flop-over comb in the female was to be found in many countries of Europe. Old breeds such as the Belgian Brakel, Pheasant Fowls and the Scots Grey had similar features such as white ear lobes, flop-over combs and laid white eggs. It is possible therefore that this Mediterranean type was the original fowl of Europe and that the heavier type of Leghorn evident today was due to crossing Malays, Cochins and Minorcas. Prolific layers of white eggs, Leghorns are a light, soft-feathered breed and non sitters. There are now other colour variations available such as black, barred, buff, cuckoo, mottled and partridge, and bantams are miniatures of their large fowl counterparts.

MALAY

The Malay originated in Asia and was one of the first breeds introduced into Britain around 1830. It was developed in Cornwall and Devon and was one of the first to be developed as a bantam. Nowadays they are one of the largest bantam breeds, very tall and upright looking with long yellow legs. Colour variations include black, white, pyle and spangled.

MARANS

This is a hen from Marans in France which was introduced to Britain in 1929. It is a heavy breed and is the one breed where it is relatively easy to distinguish male and female chicks – males have a white spot on the top of their heads while females have a darker one. They lay very large deep brown eggs and are a good choice of breed for free-range as they forage well. Bantams are available as miniatures of their large fowl counterparts.

MARSH DAISY

A rare British breed which was popular in the 1920s. It was created in the 1880s by a Mr Wright in Southport. Old English Game, Malays, Hamburghs, Leghorns and Sicilian Buttercups were used in the creation of the breed. Colours vary from white and black to wheaten and buff. They are good foragers, go broody easily and are good mothers, laying tinted eggs.

MINORCA

The Minorca probably originated in Spain and used to be very popular since it was a prolific layer of very large white eggs. Minorcas have large white ear lobes and there are black and white versions. The hen has a large single comb which drops down over her face.

MODERN GAME

Developed from Malay crosses, and similarly upstanding with long legs, Modern Game come in 13 different colours.

NANKIN

Now a rare breed, the Nankin is a true bantam which originated in Java and parts of India. The cock and hen are ginger-buff in colour, but the hen should be lighter and has short legs.

NEW HAMPSHIRE RED

New Hampshire Reds were bred by selection using Rhode Island Reds in New Hampshire, America and standardised in 1935. No other breed was used in the breeding process. As the name suggests, they are a reddish brown colour with a single comb and yellow legs; they lay light brown eggs.

OLD ENGLISH GAME

There are two varieties of Old English Game: Carlisle and Oxford. In general these Old Game varieties were used for cock-fighting, probably from Roman times right up until 1849 when an Act of Parliament made cock-fighting illegal. It was after this that many breeders began to exhibit Game fowl which have been bred in a multitude of colours. They are a hard-feathered breed, and are tall and slim with long legs. Bantam versions also come in a huge variety of colours. They are small and lay cream eggs but are used more as show birds than for their egg laying abilities.

OLD ENGLISH PHEASANT FOWL

This is an old English Breed originally called Yorkshire or Golden Pheasant. It is a light breed with a rose comb and there are gold or silver varieties. The hens lay white eggs.

ORLOFF

This breed originated in Iran. Some were taken to Moscow and re-named by Count Orloff Techesmensky. From Russia they were introduced to Britain, Holland and Germany in the late 1800s. Bantam versions were not recognised in Britain until the Seventies. The Orloff's main characteristic is the muffling around its neck; there are black, cuckoo, mahogany, spangled and white varieties.

ORPINGTON

Orpington fowl were named after a village in Kent where William Cook first bred them in the late 1800s. The black variety was followed by the white and then the buff. There is now a blue variety as well. Orpingtons are compact with short legs and classified as a heavy soft-feathered breed. Bantams are also available in this breed and are very popular as they are docile and good with children. The Queen Mother used to keep large fowl Buff Orpingtons. The Black Orpington was re-introduced to this country from Australia in the Twenties and called the Australorp. A later introduction was the Jubilee Orpington, which is rarely seen but has recently been added to the breeds at the Domestic Fowl Trust.

PEKIN

The Pekin was introduced to Britain from China. In 1860 the summer palace of the Chinese Emperor at Pekin was sacked by English and French forces and some Pekin Bantams were brought home to England as plunder. The Pekin was originally thought to be a miniature of the Cochin, but in reality has no connection with it. Pekins are a genuine bantam breed and are small with feathered feet and are a wonderful tame breed for children. They come in a variety of colours including black, blue, white, cuckoo, lavender and partridge.

PLYMOUTH ROCK

This breed originated in America and sadly the large white variety is used in the world's broiler breeding stocks. Bantam versions are available in various colours, but buff and barred bantams are the most popular. This heavy soft-feathered breed make excellent layers.

POLAND

The Poland, a light breed which originated in Europe, has an amazing crest to distinguish it. Colour variations include white-crested black, black, white, gold, silver, chamois and white crested blue. Poland bantams are also available and they lay white eggs.

RHODE ISLAND RED

This is a well known breed that originated in America, bred on farms of Rhode Island Province. The breed is used extensively in crossings and the male, being a gold, is used in gold-silver sex linked matings. The breed was imported to Britain around 1900. It has yellow skin and legs, is a heavy breed, lays very well, does not go broody easily and the eggs vary from light to dark brown.

ROSECOMB BANTAM

Only available as a bantam, the Rosecomb originated in Asia. It is small but sprightly with distinctive large white ear lobes and a rose comb. The wings are carried low and the breed comes in black, blue and white varieties. These bantams are mainly used for showing.

SABELPOOT (Booted Bantam)

This is a rare breed of bantam from Holland. It was crossed with the Barbu D'Anvers to produce the Barbu D'Uccle, which it resembles, except that it has no muffling. It lays tinted eggs.

SCOTS DUMPY

These hens are so short they appear to have no legs and waddle around rather like ducks. They are an ancient breed from Scotland, laying small tinted eggs with huge yolks. The Scots Dumpy is a light soft-feathered breed, an excellent sitter and good mother. It is a Rare Breed Survival Trust's listed breed.

SCOTS GREY

An old breed, the Scots Grey was used on the isolated crofts in Scotland to provide meat and eggs. It is a light non-sitting breed but quite rare today outside Scotland. The steel grey colour with metallic black barring is distinctive. The Scots Grey is also a listed breed.

SEBRIGHT

The Sebright is a true bantam originating in Britain, and there are two types: gold and silver. They're very pretty, small long bodied bantams, with wings carried low and tails carried high. They have a rose comb and lay cream coloured eggs. The cock does not have any hackles so is referred to as 'hen-feathered'.

SICILIAN BUTTERCUP

You can't miss a Sicilian Buttercup, which has an amazing saucer-shaped cup comb. Imported to Britain in 1912 by Mrs Colbeck of Yorkshire as a good layer of white eggs and needing little food, it was popular in the Sixties but is now rare. It is only available in gold or silver.

SILKIE

Silkies originated in Asia, some think in India, others think in China or Japan. They are famous for their broodiness and are covered in fine, silky fluff rather than feathers. Silkies are crested with feathers on the legs and five toes. Colours range from blue, gold, black, white and partridge. Ear lobes should rightly be turquoise and comb and wattles mulberry. Silkies are classified as a light soft-feathered large fowl but a small bantam version has been created which is docile and therefore popular with children.

SUSSEX

This is an old breed derived from the Old Sussex fowls which were bred in Victorian times for their meat and eggs. The oldest variety is the Speckled Sussex. Brahma, Cochin and Dorking were used to breed the Light Sussex, which is widely kept nowadays by standard and commercial breeders. It is a heavy soft-feathered breed which lays tinted eggs. There are also buff, brown and red varieties and a recent type, the Silver Sussex . All are available as bantams as well. The Light Sussex hen is one of our most popular breeds for producing table birds.

TRANSYLVANIAN NAKED NECK

This breed originated in Hungary in an area which is now in Romania. Noted for its sparseness of feathers, with none on its bright red neck, it is rather an ugly bird but hardy; an excellent forager and a good layer. Due to its likeness to a turkey it has been known as Churkey. In France they are, to their misfortune, one of the main breeds for the broiler industry.

WELSUMMER

Welsummers originated in Holland, named after the village of Welsum. A light, soft-feathered breed, they lay large brown eggs with a matt shell rather than the glossy shell of the Maran.

They are not particularly good layers but are non-sitters, so do not go broody.

WYANDOTTE

The first variety of the Wyandotte was the silver-laced and it originated in America, named after a tribe of American Indians. It has been suggested that the Brahma, Hamburgh and Polish were all used to develop the Wyandotte. It was introduced into Britain in the late 1800s and in the early 1900s was very popular, along with the Leghorn, as an egg-laying breed. There are several different varieties nowadays which include gold, buff and blue-laced, partridge, columbian and silver pencilled. Varieties have been developed by crossing different breeds with Wyandottes – for example the partridge Cochin and gold-spangled Hamburgh males were crossed with silver-laced females to produce the gold-laced varieties and the columbians came about by crossing white Wyandottes with Brahmas. Wyandottes are a heavy, soft-feathered breed and lay tinted eggs.

YOKOHAMA

A rare breed from Japan noted for its very long tail, it is a beautifully stylish bird with its exotic plumage.

Other rarer breeds and their countries of origin include: Norfolk Grey, Ixworth, Lincolnshire Buff (British), Dominique, Jersey Giant (American); Phoenix, Tuzo Bantam, Ko-Shamo Bantam (Japan); North Holland Blue, Friesan, Breda (Netherlands); Lakenfelder, Vorwerk, Augsburger (Germany); Houdan, La Fleche (France); Brakel (Belgium); Appenzeller (Switzerland); Fayoumi (Egypt); Sultan (Turkey); Sumatra (Sumatra) and Asil (a Game variety from India).

9. SOME OF THE PROBLEMS AND DISEASES

First of all, preventative steps can be made so that you are less likely to encounter disease and external and internal parasites that can make your hen's life a misery: keep your hen houses clean and the drinking water clean and fresh; do not leave uneaten food hanging around for too long or before you know it you will be invaded with rats and mice; disinfecting your hen house every three months can help prevent red mite. The more free-range your bantams or hens are, the less likely they are going to be beset by any diseases.

Using a vet can be quite uneconomic because a visit can often prove more expensive that the original cost of the hen but if your sick hen is a valued pet then you may have no choice.

When you handle your hen to check her over, you should hold her in your left hand with her body on your palm and forearm so that you can hold her legs with your fingers.

There follows information on some of the more common ailments, problems and diseases, but this is only intended as a very rough guide.

Common Problems

Crop Bound
The crop will hang down heavily. If you pick the hen up you will feel a hard ball of food which has accumulated within – often this is a twisted ball of grass. Pour a little olive oil down her throat and if you gently massage the crop, the food should soften and pass through. Alternatively you could give the hen a drink of warm water, then turn her upside down and gently

massage the crop to try and release the blockage.

Overgrown Beak
The top part of the beak may grow much longer than the bottom part. You can resolve this problem by cutting back the top part with a sharp pair of scissors so that it is level.

Worms
There are six different types of worms which can live in the internal parts of chickens. Your hens infected with worms will be listless and have green diarrhoea. You should treat for worms with Flubenvet (available from feed suppliers) mixed into the feed. However some authorities say that you should treat for worms twice a year whether your hens show symptoms or not and some say that de-worming a healthy hen weakens the system and upsets the natural balance of helpful organisms.

Bumblefoot
This can be caused by a chicken damaging its foot when it jumps down from a perch which is too high. There will be a round swelling which looks not unlike a corn or wart on the pad of the foot.

Diseases

Colds
The common cold can affect your hens or bantams and is often due to bad ventilation or cold conditions. There will be discharge from the nostrils and sneezing. Isolate the birds affected and sponge their faces gently with warm water and dose with a little cod liver oil.

Mycoplasma Infection
This starts with sneezing and coughing, a runny nose and eyes, and you may hear a rasping noise in the affected bird's

breathing. This respiratory infection is treatable with an injection of Tylan 200.

Infectious Bronchitis
The symptoms for bronchitis are similar to that of a cold. There will also be a decrease in egg production and the oviduct will be permanently damaged resulting in a future of soft-shelled eggs.

Coccidiosis
This disease is caused by the Coccidia parasite. Symptoms will include listlessness with head sunk into the neck, white diarrhoea and sometimes blood in the droppings. Treat with Proleth in the drinking water.

Aspergillosis
This is a type of pneumonia which may break out in chicks. It involves a species of fungus found in mouldy litter or stale food. Birds affected will appear unsteady on their feet and will be gasping and breathing heavily. There is no cure and infected chicks should be humanely killed.

Heart Disease
This will be evident in old hens or bantams and the most obvious sign will be a purple comb and loss of energy. There is no treatment.

External Parasites

Scaly Leg
The scaly leg mite lives under the scales of the bird's leg. It is contagious and can be seen in birds of all ages. It may originate from the litter on the floor of your hen house. The scales on the legs become rough, and a chalk-like concretion is formed, which accumulates both between and over the scales. It is

intensely irritating to the bird and once developed may make the bird lame and unable to perch. The problem is relatively easy to cure and there are several different treatments you can try. In the past I have used surgical spirit, which you can paint on the legs with a small paintbrush once a week for five weeks. Other treatments include scaly cream which is available in pet shops (used for budgies with scaly face); Eucalyptus oil which is an organic treatment and must be rubbed into the legs every few weeks; paraffin (an old fashioned remedy) with which you can scrub the legs using an old toothbrush (one treatment should be enough); dipping the legs in linseed oil, which reduces the irritation, softens the scales and promotes healing but you need to repeat this treatment; Vaseline or petroleum jelly gently rubbed into the legs but you will need to repeat this treatment; and lastly for severe cases of scaly leg use Protocon (sulphur based ointment) which you must cover the legs with, then wrap in paper tissue and use tape to keep it in place, leave for at least a week and then you should find the scabs will drop off.

Red Mites
Red mites live and breed in crevices in hen houses. They are carried by wild birds. At night they run along the perches and up the chicken's leg where they suck blood from the flesh. They don't live on the bird but can be spotted during the day – they will be red if they have recently sucked blood, otherwise they will be grey. The chickens affected will look jaundiced through losing blood and will stop laying. Creosoting of the hen houses will also prevent the establishment of red mite. There are sprays available to kill them.

Lice (fleas)
These are irritating for the bird and can be treated by dousing the birds with louse powder. You can also dust the nest boxes and dust baths with the powder. Broody hens should also be dusted with powder before sitting.

10. THE EGG

Composition

An egg consists of five parts – the germinal disc or blastodisc (inside the yolk), the yolk, the albumen (white part), the shell membrane or skin and the shell. There is also an air pocket which increases in size as the egg ages and the chalazae are twisted bands of protein which hold the yolk in place.

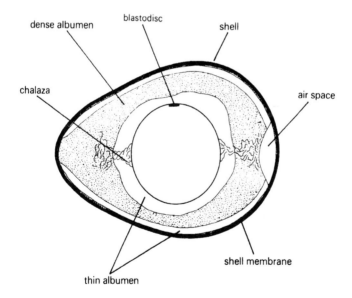

dense albumen

blastodisc

shell

chalaza

air space

thin albumen

shell membrane

Picture of egg

Overall the chemical composition of an entire egg is about 69% water, 11% protein, 10% fat, 1% ash (mineral substances) and the shell constitutes the remaining 9%. Eggs are especially valuable as a source of protein – they are one of the highest quality protein-rich foods occurring naturally. The yolk contains Vitamins A, B (thiamine, riboflavin and niacin) D and E but no vitamin C. Egg yolks are one of the few foods naturally containing Vitamin D. The egg contains iron, phosphorus and iodine but is low in calcium, which is all in the shell. There is more unsaturated than saturated fat. An average egg contains about 76 calories.

Some research has been done into the nutritional values of a free-range egg with a deep yellow yolk against a battery egg – free-range eggs were found to have considerably more Vitamin B12 and folic acid. It might also be mentioned here that your free-range egg yolks will be naturally yellow from the pigment that your hen has obtained naturally. Commercial poultry keepers do often include pigments in the feed to artificially make the egg yolks yellower.

A fertile egg has a tiny white speck on the edge of the yolk. This does not affect the taste of the egg.

If you break an egg and the white looks cloudy, don't worry - this is actually a sign of freshness not age.

The shell is largely composed of calcium carbonate and has thousands of tiny pores over its surface. Through this porous shell the egg can absorb flavours and smells. When an egg is laid it is slightly moist (the cuticle) but this film quickly dries. This is a protective coat for the egg. If it is washed away, micro-organisms may penetrate through the pores in the shell and infect the egg. This is why it is best, if possible, not to wash freshly laid eggs.

Storing Eggs

You should keep your eggs in the fridge in egg boxes to prevent them absorbing the flavours of other foods; you should bring them out about half an hour before they are to be used so they are at room temperature. Alternatively just keep your eggs in a cool place but away from other foods.

Your eggs need to be as fresh as possible if you want fried or poached eggs. For boiled eggs that you wish to peel, it is best to use eggs that are about a week old as the shell and skin are really difficult to peel off on fresh eggs. The skin is the membrane that would have protected the chick if the egg had been fertilised. It is very taut and stretched on a fresh egg but slackens off as air penetrates the shell as the days go by. If you are scrambling your eggs or making an omelette, eggs can be up to a week old. For baked dishes, eggs can be older than a week. If you want to separate the yolks and whites to make meringues, eggs are best a few days old as the whites whisk up better if not too fresh.

You can test how fresh your eggs are by submerging each one in a glass of cold water. An egg that lies horizontally at the bottom is fresh. One that tilts up slightly could be a week old. One that floats into a vertical position is stale but could still be used in a baked dish, and one that floats to the surface has definitely gone bad.

You will know from when you eat a boiled egg that there is a gap or an air-pocket inside between the white of the egg and the shell. This air-pocket increases as the egg gets older. A newly laid egg will have virtually no air inside but as the shell is porous, this means that gradually the air will increase inside the egg. If you break an egg onto a plate you can also see how fresh it is – if the yolk stands plump and upright and the egg white does the same round the yolk then the egg is very fresh.

A stale egg will look much flatter with a watery white spreading out round the yolk.

If you are separating your eggs and wish to use only the whites, you can store the yolks in the fridge for up to two days covered with a little water to prevent a skin forming. Alternatively, if you are using the yolks, you can store the whites in the fridge for up to a week but in this case it is best to use them in cooked dishes.

Freezing Eggs

If in the spring you find yourself inundated with eggs, you can freeze them. Raw eggs must be frozen out of their shells and you can either freeze the yolks and whites separately or together. Separate the yolks from the whites – it is important that for this method the eggs are very fresh as stale yolks are liable to break and you don't want yolk in the egg white. Add either a little salt or a little sugar to the yolks and freeze in a suitable container. Whites can be frozen as they are, but cooked whites do not freeze well. Cooked yolks are okay frozen if incorporated into another dish. Whole raw eggs frozen in small containers can be fried or poached straight from the freezer.

Storage in Waterglass

Storing eggs in waterglass is an old method of preserving eggs which may be of interest. You can store eggs for up to a year by putting them in waterglass solution (soluble sodium silicate). This seals the pores in the shell preventing the loss of moisture from the inside and keeps out bacteria. In other words, by storing eggs in waterglass you are making their shells impervious. You should only use fresh, unwashed, uncracked eggs. Sodium silicate can be bought as a concentrated solution in a tin in the chemist. It may be difficult to find as the demand is not great nowadays but try old fashioned chemists or ironmongers – a 300ml, ½pt tin of sodium silicate will be enough to preserve 80 eggs. You should mix the sodium silicate powder with an equal part in weight of water and then this solution is diluted by one part to 20 parts of water. Earthenware jars or enamel buckets are the best containers to use. Fill with the solution and place the eggs carefully in the container, broad end uppermost with about 5cm, 2in of solution above the eggs. You should cover the container and since water will evaporate you will need occasionally to top up the solution. When you want to use any eggs, wash them thoroughly under running cold water and prick them with a pin if you want to boil them.

Pickling Eggs

You could try pickling surplus eggs. First you need to hard-boil them. For about 14 hard-boiled eggs you need 900ml, 1½pt of white wine vinegar. Simmer the vinegar with a small piece of root ginger and a tablespoon of white peppercorns for about 15 minutes. Allow to cool and strain. Peel the eggs and arrange in a large glass jar. Add one red chilli pepper and then pour on the spiced vinegar. Seal and leave for a couple of weeks before using.

SECTION TWO

EGG RECIPES

Cook's Note: Your eggs may vary in weight. Recipes are based on an average egg weighing 50g, 2oz. For recipes requiring a Swiss roll tin this should measure 33 x 23cm (13 x 9in).

EGGS COOKED ON THEIR OWN

BOILED EGGS

Eggs should be at room temperature and should be put gently in a pan of simmering water. If you want softly boiled eggs, small ones should only take 4 minutes and larger ones 5 minutes. Hard-boiled eggs will take between 8 and 10 minutes.

POACHED EGGS

If you do not have an egg poacher use a shallow frying pan filled with 3.5cm, 1½in of water and heat until simmering. Break the eggs into a saucer and then carefully slide into the water. Cook for 3 minutes and remove with a fish slice.

BAKED EGGS

These are eggs baked in little dishes called cocottes or any little ramekin dishes. Break the eggs into the little greased dishes and place in a roasting tin half filled with water. Add a little knob of butter to each egg and bake for about 8 minutes at gas mark 4, 180°C (350°F).

CODDLED EGGS

These are very soft eggs steamed in egg coddlers. Break the egg into the coddler and screw or clip the lid on. Place in simmering water in a saucepan so that the water comes three quarters of the way up the side. Then turn off the heat and leave for about 8 minutes.

FRIED EGGS

Heat a little butter or olive oil in a frying pan and add the egg or eggs. Baste frequently until the yolk is set – serve 'sunny side up' or flip over so that the yolk becomes encased by some of the white.

SCRAMBLED EGGS

For two people use four eggs. Break them into a bowl and whisk well with a fork. Melt a little butter in a small saucepan. Add the eggs and stir with a wooden spoon until just setting. Do not overdo the eggs.

OMELETTES

For a plain omelette use two eggs per person. Break into a bowl and whisk up with a fork. Add a little single cream if liked and a seasoning of salt and pepper. Heat butter or oil in a frying pan and tip the egg in, tilting the pan from side to side so that the egg spreads out evenly, and keep tilting the pan so that any liquid egg can cook. Lift a part of the omelette with a fish slice to see if it is cooked underneath and then fold one half on top of the other half – cook for a another minute or so and serve immediately.

SAVOURY RECIPES

EGG AND LEMON SOUP

Serves 6

1.2 litres, 2pt chicken stock
100g, 4oz long grain rice
2 tbsp parsley, chopped
salt and pepper
3 eggs
3 tbsp lemon juice
sliced lemon and parsley to garnish
50g, 2oz bread croutons

Pour the stock into a large saucepan and, bringing it to the boil, stir in the rice. Simmer gently for 15 minutes. Stir in the parsley and seasoning. Beat the eggs in a separate bowl with the lemon juice and stir in a spoonful of the soup. Carefully pour the egg mixture into the soup and stir continuously without boiling until the soup thickens. Garnish with sliced lemon and the parsley and serve with bread croutons.

EGG AND ANCHOVY MOUSSE

Serves 6

8 eggs, hard-boiled
1 small can of anchovies
300ml, ½pt vegetable stock
15g, ½oz gelatine
150ml, ¼pt double cream, whipped
1 tsp Worcestershire sauce
salt and pepper

Mash the eggs up and add about 6 of the anchovy fillets, sliced finely. Soak the gelatine in 3 tablespoons of stock. Add the rest of the stock and warm gently until the gelatine has dissolved. Pour at once onto the egg mixture. Add the whipped cream and Worcestershire sauce. Pour into a 1 litre, 2 pint mould and chill until set. Turn out and lay the remaining anchovy fillets on top.

EGG AND SALMON MOUSSE

Serves 6 as a starter

300ml, ½pt milk
1 bay leaf
1 onion, stuck with 2 cloves
1 small carrot
15g, ½oz gelatine dissolved in 2 tbsp water
150ml, ¼pt dry white wine
3 hard-boiled eggs
40g, 1½oz butter
25g, 1oz flour
2 eggs, separated
1 x 200g, 8oz tin of red salmon, drained
3 tbsp single cream

Heat the milk gently in a saucepan with the bay leaf, onion and carrot and leave to infuse for 20 minutes. Add the dissolved gelatine to the wine and pour a little onto the base of a 900ml, 1½pt mould. Leave to set. Slice the hard-boiled eggs and arrange the slices on top of the gelatine, pouring a little more of the gelatine mixture over them. Meanwhile strain the milk. Melt the butter in a saucepan, stir in the flour and gradually add the milk. Stir until you have a smooth sauce. Beat in the egg yolks and then add the salmon. Transfer to a food processor and whiz up with the remaining gelatine mixture and the cream. Whisk the egg whites until stiff and fold into the mixture. Turn into the mould and chill for at least a couple of hours. Turn out and serve garnished with lemon slices.

FLAMENCO EGGS

Serves 4

1 tbsp olive oil
1 onion, peeled and sliced
1 clove of garlic, peeled and crushed
1 red pepper, deseeded and sliced
1 x 400g, 1lb tin of tomatoes
50g, 2oz peas
50g, 2oz French beans
50g, 2oz chorizo sausage, thinly sliced
4 eggs
½ tsp paprika and some chopped parsley

Fry the onion, garlic and red pepper in the oil until soft. Add the tomatoes, peas, beans and sausage. Cook for a couple of minutes. Spoon into 4 individual shallow gratin dishes and break an egg into the centre of each one. Sprinkle with paprika and parsley. Bake in the oven at gas mark 6, 200°C (400°F) for about 15 minutes or until the eggs are set. Serve with hot rolls or bread.

SPANISH TORTILLA

Serves 3 - 4

4 tbsp olive oil
450g, 1lb potatoes, such as Maris Piper, peeled and diced
2 onions, peeled and sliced
6 eggs
salt and pepper

Heat the oil in a frying pan and add the diced potatoes. Cook for several minutes and then add the onion. Beat the eggs together. Add them to the pan and cook over a low heat until the eggs are set. Season and turn out onto a serving plate.

71

OMELETTE ARNOLD BENNETT

Serves 2

25g, 1oz butter
2 tbsp single cream
100g, 4oz smoked haddock, cooked and flaked
3 eggs, separated
50g, 2oz grated Cheddar cheese
1 tbsp olive oil

Melt the butter and stir in the cream and the fish. Stir the egg yolks in to the mixture. Whisk the egg whites and fold them in with half the cheese. Heat the oil in a frying pan and add the fish mixture, spreading it out evenly. Cook until beginning to set. Sprinkle the rest of the cheese over the omelette and finish under the grill. Serve at once.

SCRAMBLED EGGS WITH ONION AND BACON

Serves 4

15g, ½oz butter
8 spring onions, chopped
4 bacon rashers, chopped into small pieces
8 eggs, beaten
1 tbsp single cream
grinding of black pepper
chopped parsley

Melt the butter in a small saucepan and add the onions and bacon pieces. Fry until soft and then add the eggs and cook gently while continuing to stir until they scramble. Mix in the tablespoon of cream and season with pepper and parsley.

BAKED EGGS WITH SMOKED SALMON

Serves 4

Butter for greasing
100g, 4oz smoked salmon
4 eggs
200ml, 7fl oz single cream
fresh parsley, chopped

Butter 4 ramekin dishes and cover the bottoms with strips of smoked salmon. Break an egg into each ramekin and divide the cream between them. Place in a frying pan half filled with simmering water and cook over a gentle heat for about 6 minutes or until the whites are firm. Sprinkle with parsley and serve.

PIPERADE

Serves 2

A piperade is a dish of eggs and vegetables, traditionally peppers and tomatoes.

50g, 2oz butter
1 onion, peeled and chopped
2 cloves of garlic, peeled and chopped
2 red peppers, deseeded and sliced
3 tomatoes, chopped
4 eggs
1 tbsp fresh parsley, chopped

Melt the butter in a pan and add the onion and garlic. Then add the peppers and tomatoes and sauté gently until soft. Whisk up the eggs and add to the vegetables with the parsley. Cook for a further 4 or 5 minutes. Serve at once, perhaps on toast or accompanied by some croutons.

EGGS BENEDICT

Serves 4

2 muffins, halved
butter
4 eggs
4 slices ham

4 tbsp Hollandaise sauce

Toast the muffins and spread each half with butter. Poach the eggs. Lay a slice of ham on each half muffin, followed by an egg. Drizzle a spoonful of Hollandaise sauce over each egg and serve immediately.

FLORENTINE EGGS

Serves 4

450g, 1lb fresh spinach, stalks removed
4 spring onions, chopped
4 slices ham
4 eggs
2 tbsp single cream

Cook the spinach for a couple of minutes in a covered saucepan so that it wilts. Line 4 gratin dishes with the spinach. Arrange the ham and spring onions on top and crack an egg into the centre of each one. Top each one with a little cream. Place the dishes in a roasting tin half filled with boiling water and bake at gas mark 5, 190°C (375°F) for 20 minutes. Serve with hot rolls.

RATATOUILLE WITH TUNA AND EGGS

Serves 4

3 tbsp olive oil
1 small aubergine, sliced
1 green pepper, deseeded and sliced
1 red onion, peeled and sliced
2 courgettes, sliced
2 cloves of garlic, peeled and crushed
1 x 400g, 1lb tin of tomatoes
2 tbsp tomato purée
150ml, ¼pt water
200g, 7oz tin of tuna chunks, drained
4 eggs

Heat the oil in a frying pan and add the aubergine, pepper, onion, courgette and garlic. Cook for several minutes to soften the vegetables. Add the tin of tomatoes, the tomato purée and the water. Simmer gently for 30 minutes. Stir in the tuna. Make 4 wells in the mixture and crack the eggs into the wells. Place under the grill to cook the eggs. Serve with crusty bread or rolls.

SPINACH, EGG AND HAM PIE

Serves 6

250g, 9oz shortcrust pastry
1 onion, peeled and sliced
1 clove of garlic, peeled and crushed
2 tbsp olive oil
275g, 10oz spinach
225g, 8oz ham
225g, 8oz mozzarella cheese, sliced
1 red pepper, deseeded and chopped
4 eggs, beaten

Roll the pastry into two rounds, one slightly bigger than the other. Line a greased 20cm, 8in pie dish with the bigger round and keep the other round for the lid. Sauté the onion and garlic in the oil. Cook the spinach for a few minutes in a little water and then drain and chop it before stirring it into the onion mixture. Lay slices of ham on the pastry base. Cover with the mozzarella. Lay the spinach mixture on top and sprinkle on the chopped red pepper. Pour the beaten eggs over the top reserving a little. Cover with the pastry lid, brush with the reserved egg and cut slits in the pastry. Bake in the oven at gas mark 6, 200°C (400°F) for 35 minutes, or until golden on top.

SPINACH ROULADE

Serves 3 - 4

700g,1½lb fresh spinach, washed
4 eggs, separated
pinch of nutmeg

Cheese sauce

40g, 1½oz butter
25g, 1oz flour
300ml, ½pt milk
100g, 4oz mature Cheddar cheese, grated
cayenne pepper

To make the roulade, cook the spinach without any water in a covered saucepan for a few minutes. Drain off any liquid that has formed and chop finely. Mix the egg yolks with the spinach and season with nutmeg. Whisk the egg whites until they form soft peaks. Stir one tablespoon of egg white into the spinach mixture and then fold in the rest in two batches. Pour this mixture into a lined, greased Swiss roll tin and bake in the oven at gas mark 6, 200°C (400°F) for 10 minutes. Turn the roulade out onto a clean sheet of greaseproof paper and peel off the lining paper. Make the cheese sauce by melting the butter, stirring in the flour and gradually adding the milk. Stir until smooth and mix in half the grated cheese. Spread some of the cheese sauce over the roulade and roll up carefully. Don't worry if it cracks a little – this is normal. Pour the remaining cheese sauce over the top and sprinkle with the remaining grated cheese and a little cayenne pepper. Return to the oven for 5 minutes so that the cheese melts. Serve immediately.

RECIPES USING BOILED EGGS

EGG PATÉ

Serves 8 as a starter

1 tbsp gelatine dissolved in 2 tbsp of water
450g, 1lb can consommé
150ml, ¼pt double cream
6 eggs, hard-boiled and chopped
150ml, ¼pt crème fraîche

Pour the consommé into a bowl and add the gelatine. Whip the cream and fold in the chopped eggs, crème fraîche and almost all the consommé. Divide the mixture between 8 ramekin dishes and leave to set. Reheat the reserved consommé and spoon over the tops of the patés. Garnish with lemon slices and chives.

TUNA STUFFED EGGS

Serves 4 – 6

6 eggs, hard-boiled
100g, 4oz tinned tuna, drained
1 tbsp fresh parsley, chopped
1 tbsp mayonnaise
1 clove of garlic, crushed
½ tbsp capers, chopped

Cut the eggs in half and remove the yolks. Mash them with the tuna and mix in all the other ingredients until you have a paste. Fill the egg halves with this mixture and serve as an hors d'oeuvre.

SCOTCH EGGS

Serves 4

4 eggs, hard-boiled
225g, 8oz sausagemeat
1 tsp dried chopped sage
pinch of mace
1 medium onion, peeled and finely chopped
grated lemon rind from half a lemon
2 eggs, beaten
2 tbsp flour
100g, 4oz brown breadcrumbs
oil for deep frying

Fry the onions in a little butter but do not allow to brown. Mix the sausagemeat with the chopped sage, mace, onion and grated lemon rind. Divide the sausagemeat into four. Now mould each piece of sausagemeat round the egg, using your hands, until you have completely enclosed it. Next, dip each Scotch egg in some of the flour, then in the egg, repeat and then roll in the breadcrumbs. Deep fry the Scotch eggs until well browned on all sides. Halve each one and eat hot or cold.

CREAMY EGG CURRY

Serves 4 – 6

3 tbsp olive oil
1 onion, peeled and chopped
2.5cm, 1in piece of fresh ginger, peeled and grated
1 green chilli, seeded and chopped
600ml, 1pt single cream
1 tbsp lemon juice
1 tsp cumin seeds
pinch of cayenne pepper
1 tsp garam masala
1 tbsp tomato purée
150ml, ¼pt vegetable stock
12 eggs, hard-boiled
3 tbsp fresh coriander, chopped

Heat the oil in a large frying pan and fry the onion for a few minutes. Add the ginger, chilli and all the other ingredients except the eggs and coriander. Bring up to a simmer. Then halve the eggs, add them to the sauce and cook for 5 minutes, stirring the sauce if it sticks to the bottom of the pan. When ready to serve transfer to a serving dish, sprinkle with the coriander and serve with boiled basmati rice and mango chutney.

CHEESY EGG, BACON AND RICE DISH

Serves 4 – 6

2 tbsp olive oil
1 onion, peeled and chopped
150g, 5oz back bacon
225g, 8oz long grain brown rice
600ml, 1pt vegetable stock
3 eggs, hard-boiled
15g, ½oz butter
1 tbsp flour
150ml, ¼pt milk
75g, 3oz mature Cheddar cheese
2 tbsp brown breadcrumbs
pinch of cayenne pepper (optional)

Heat the oil in a casserole and soften the onion. Chop the bacon and add to the onion. Fry for 5 minutes, then add the rice and stir to coat it in the oil. Add the stock, cover and simmer for 40 minutes. Slice the eggs and spread over the top of the rice. Make the sauce by melting the butter, stirring in the flour and gradually adding the milk. Stir until smooth and pour over the eggs. Sprinkle the cheese, breadcrumbs and cayenne pepper over the sauce and put under a hot grill for a couple of minutes to brown the top. Serve at once with garlic bread and a salad.

SALADE NICOISE

There are many versions of this classic French salad.

Serves 6

Handful of salad leaves
150g, 5oz French beans
½ cucumber, cut into sticks
1 red onion, peeled and sliced thinly
6 eggs, hard-boiled
200g, 7oz tin of tuna steaks in oil, drained
handful of cherry tomatoes, halved
50g, 2oz tin of anchovies
50g, 2oz black olives

Dressing

5 tbsp olive oil
1 tbsp balsamic vinegar
1 clove of garlic, peeled and crushed
salt and pepper

First cook the French beans in boiling water for 3 or 4 minutes, drain and put under cold running water to retain their green colour. Arrange the salad leaves in a bowl and spread the beans, onion and cucumber over them. Halve the boiled eggs and add to the salad along with the tuna, tomatoes, anchovies and olives. For the dressing stir together the oil, vinegar, garlic and salt and pepper and pour over the salad.

KEDGEREE

Serves 4

450g, 1lb smoked haddock
150ml, ¼pt milk
225g, 8oz basmati rice
4 eggs, hard-boiled
handful of fresh chives and parsley

Gently heat the smoked haddock in the milk and cook for a few minutes. Drain the haddock and flake, reserving the milk. Cook the rice as per the packet instructions. Add the haddock to the rice and stir in the milk, hard-boiled eggs, cream and herbs.

POTATO AND EGG SALAD

Serves 4

450g, 1lb new potatoes, cooked
2 tbsp olive oil
1 tsp white wine vinegar
4 spring onions, sliced
4 eggs, hard-boiled and sliced
4 tbsp mayonnaise
1 tbsp fresh chives, chopped

Chop up the potatoes and while still warm add the olive oil and vinegar. Mix in the spring onions and eggs. Stir in the mayonnaise and sprinkle with chopped chives.

TARTS

QUICHE LORRAINE

Serves 6

175g, 6oz shortcrust pastry

25g, 1oz butter
1 onion, peeled and chopped
175g, 6oz unsmoked bacon, chopped
100g, 4oz mature Cheddar cheese, grated
3 eggs
200ml, 7fl oz single cream

Roll out the pastry and use to line a greased 20cm, 8in flan dish. Prick the base and cook in the oven at gas mark 4, 180°C (350°F) for 15 minutes. Meanwhile melt the butter in a frying pan and fry the onion and bacon until crisp. Transfer to the cooked pastry shell. Sprinkle the grated cheese over the bacon mixture. Whisk together the eggs and cream and pour over the bacon and cheese. Cook in the oven for a further 25 minutes until golden brown and set.

THREE CHEESE AND CHIVE TART

Serves 6

Cheese pastry

150g, 5oz plain flour
75g, 3oz butter
25g, 1oz mature Cheddar cheese, grated
1 egg yolk

For the filling

3 eggs
100g, 4oz Ricotta cheese
3 tbsp crème fraîche
2 tbsp fresh chives, chopped
225g, 8oz goat's cheese with rind

To make the pastry mix the butter into the flour using your fingertips until the mixture resembles breadcrumbs. Mix in the cheese and bind together with the egg yolk and a little water. Roll out the pastry and use to line a greased 23cm, 9in flan dish with the pastry and bake blind for 15 minutes. Whisk the eggs and Ricotta together. Mix in the crème fraîche and chives. Season with pepper and a pinch of nutmeg. Pour into the pastry case and crumble the goat's cheese evenly over the mixture. Bake in the oven at gas mark 4, 180°C (350°F) for 25 minutes.

SMOKED SALMON TART

Serves 4

125g, 4½oz shortcrust pastry

For the filling

3 eggs
150ml, ¼pt single cream
150ml, ¼pt milk
15g, ½oz butter
100g, 4oz smoked salmon

Roll out the pastry and use to line a 17.5cm, 7in flan dish. Prick the pastry and bake blind in the oven at gas mark 4, 180°C (350°F) for 10 minutes. Whisk together the eggs, cream and milk and pour into the pastry case. Dot with the butter and cover with thin slices of smoked salmon. Return to the oven for a further 20 minutes or until the tart is set.

MORE HOT DISHES WITH EGGS

SPAGHETTI ALLA CARBONARA

Serves 4

225g, 8oz spaghetti
4 eggs
2 tbsp single cream
225g, 8oz unsmoked bacon, chopped
100g, 4oz Parmesan or mature Cheddar cheese, grated
chopped parsley

Cook the spaghetti according to the packet instructions. Dry fry the bacon until crisp and beat the eggs together in a bowl with the cream. When you have drained the spaghetti add it to the bacon in the frying pan but with the pan off the heat. Quickly add the eggs and cream, stir them around and then add the grated cheese. Serve immediately, sprinkled with parsley.

TUNA GOUGERE

Serves 4 – 6

Choux pastry
150ml, ¼pt water
50g, 2oz butter, cut into pieces
65g, 2½oz plain flour, sifted
2 eggs, beaten
50g, 2oz Cheddar cheese, grated

For the filling
15g, ½oz butter or margarine
1 small onion, peeled and chopped
1 tbsp flour
150ml, ¼pt milk
90ml, 3fl oz stock
200g, 7oz tin of tuna, drained and flaked
5 cherry tomatoes, halved
1 tbsp breadcrumbs + 1 tbsp grated cheese

To make the choux pastry put the butter and water in a saucepan and heat slowly to melt the butter, then bring to the boil. Immediately add all the flour and beat until the mixture forms a ball. Cool slightly and then add the eggs a little at a time. Whisk the mixture until smooth and glossy. Stir in the cheese. Grease a 20cm, 8in flan dish and spoon the choux pastry in a circle around the flan dish leaving a hole in the middle. For the filling, melt the butter or margarine in a saucepan and add the onion. Cook for 2 or 3 minutes and then stir in the flour. Gradually add the milk and stock until you have a smooth sauce. Mix in the tuna and tomatoes and spoon into the centre of the flan dish. Sprinkle the breadcrumbs and cheese over the filling and cook in a pre-heated oven at gas mark 6, 200°C (400°F) for 40 minutes or until the pastry is golden brown.

EGG AND PRAWN FRIED RICE

Serves 3 – 4

3 tbsp sunflower oil
4 spring onions, chopped
1 red pepper, deseeded and diced
150g, 5oz long grain rice, cooked
100g, 4oz prawns, shelled
2 tbsp soya sauce
3 eggs

Heat the oil in a wok and fry the spring onions and red pepper. Add the rice and prawns. Beat the eggs with the soya sauce and when the rice is heated through and beginning to crisp a little remove from the heat and pour the eggs over the rice. Stir the eggs through the rice. The heat will cook the eggs – serve at once with extra soya sauce if liked.

BASIC PANCAKE MIXTURE

150ml, ¼pt milk
100g, 4oz plain flour
2 eggs
3 tbsp sunflower oil

You can either whiz up the milk, flour, eggs and oil in a food processor or put the flour in a mixing bowl, make a well in the centre and gradually beat in the egg, oil and milk. When you have a smooth batter leave covered for a couple of hours before using. For a sweeter batter you can add a tablespoon of caster sugar. For a thinner batter you can use one egg and 300ml, ½pt of milk.

SOUFFLÉS

CHEESE SOUFFLÉ

Serves 4

25g, 1oz butter
25g, 1oz plain flour
300ml, ½pt milk
100g, 4oz mature Cheddar cheese, grated
4 eggs, separated

Melt the butter in a saucepan and mix in the flour. Gradually add the milk, stirring all the time until you have a smooth roux. Remove from the heat and stir in the cheese. Then beat in the egg yolks. Whisk the egg whites and carefully fold a little into the cheese sauce. Fold in the rest, using a metal spoon. Pour into a buttered soufflé dish and bake for 30 minutes at gas mark 6, 200°C (400°F) without opening the oven door. The soufflé should be golden brown on top and well risen. Serve immediately as it will collapse about 5 minutes after coming out of the oven.

CARROT SOUFFLÉ

Serves 4

450g, 1lb carrots, peeled and chopped
25g, 1oz butter
25g, 1oz plain flour
150ml, ¼pt milk
juice of ½ lemon
4 eggs, separated

Cook the carrots and purée them. Melt the butter in a saucepan and stir in the flour. Gradually add the milk, stirring all the time until the sauce is smooth. Stir in the carrot purée, lemon juice and the egg yolks one at a time. Whisk the egg whites until stiff and with a metal spoon gently fold them into the mixture. Pour into a greased soufflé dish and cook in a preheated oven at gas mark 6, 200°C (400°F) for 35 minutes. Serve immediately.

SMOKED HADDOCK SOUFFLÉ

Serves 4

450g, 1lb smoked haddock
600ml, 1pt milk
50g, 2oz butter
50g, 2oz plain flour
50g, 2oz Cheddar cheese, grated
4 eggs, separated

Put the smoked haddock and milk in a saucepan and heat gently, then simmer for 5 minutes. Remove from the heat and allow the haddock to cool in the milk. Strain the milk and reserve for the sauce. Flake the fish and remove any bones and skin. Melt the butter in a saucepan and stir in the flour. Gradually add the reserved milk, stirring all the time until the sauce is smooth. Take off the heat and stir in the cheese. Stir in the yolks one at a time and stir in the flaked fish. Leave to cool while you whisk the egg whites until stiff and then fold them into the sauce. Pour into a greased soufflé dish and bake in a preheated oven at gas mark 6, 200°C (400°F) for 35 minutes. Serve immediately.

SWEET RECIPES

TARTS

MAPLE SYRUP AND PECAN PIE

Serves 6

Sweet Pastry

150g, 5oz plain flour
75g, 3oz butter
1 tbsp caster sugar
1 egg yolk
water

150g, 5oz pecans
4 eggs
250ml, 9fl oz maple syrup
100g, 4oz light brown sugar
50g, 2oz butter, melted
1 tsp vanilla essence

Rub the butter into the flour until the mixture resembles breadcrumbs. Stir in the sugar and bind together with the egg yolk and a little water until you have a smooth dough. Roll out and use to line a 20cm, 8in greased pie dish. Chill for 30 minutes and then prick and bake blind in a preheated oven at gas mark 4, 180°C (350°F) for 15 minutes. Arrange the pecans over the pastry base. Beat together the eggs, maple syrup, brown sugar, butter and vanilla essence. Pour over the pecans and bake in the oven at gas mark 4, 180°C (350°F) for 30 minutes. Serve with cream.

VANILLA CUSTARD TART

Serves 6

Sweet Pastry (see page 93)

For the filling

4 eggs
150ml, ¼pt single cream
150ml, ¼pt full fat milk
50g, 2oz caster sugar
½ tsp vanilla essence
freshly grated nutmeg

Roll out the pastry and use to line a 20cm, 8in greased flan dish. Chill for 30 minutes and then prick and bake blind in a preheated oven at gas mark 4, 180°C (350°F) for 15 minutes. Meanwhile prepare the custard filling. Whisk the eggs with the cream, milk, sugar and vanilla essence. Pour into the pastry case. Sprinkle nutmeg evenly over the filling. Return to the oven and cook for 20 minutes or until set.

LEMON MERINGUE PIE

Serves 6

Shortcrust pastry made with 175g, 6oz flour and 75g, 3oz
margarine
grated rind and juice of 2 lemons
40g, 1½oz cornflour
300ml, ½pt milk
2 egg yolks
100g, 4oz golden granulated sugar

Topping

2 egg whites
75g, 3oz caster sugar

Roll out the pastry and use to line a 20cm, 8in greased flan dish. Bake blind in the oven at gas mark 4, 180°C (350°F) for about 15 minutes. To prepare the filling, mix the cornflour with a little milk. Heat the remaining milk and slowly pour it onto the cornflour paste, stirring all the time. Return the mixture to the saucepan and stir in the lemon juice and rind. Bring to the boil and stir to remove any lumps. Simmer for a minute, and then beat in the granulated sugar. Beat in the egg yolks and pour into the flan case. Beat the egg whites until stiff and gradually whisk in half the caster sugar. Fold in the remaining sugar and pile on top of the lemon mixture. Bake in a preheated oven at gas mark 4, 180°C (350°F) for 15 minutes, cool slightly and serve.

APPLE AND LEMON FLAN

Serves 6

Sweet Pastry (see page 93)

3 eggs
75g, 3oz golden caster sugar
150ml, ¼pt single cream
grated rind and juice of 2 lemons
450g, 1lb cooking apples, peeled and cored
icing sugar

Roll out the pastry and use to line a 23cm, 9in greased flan dish. Chill for 30 minutes. Prick the pastry base and bake blind at gas mark 4, 180°C (350°F) for about 15 minutes. Place the eggs, cream and caster sugar in a bowl and whisk together. Add the grated lemon rind and juice and whisk until smooth. Grate the apples into the lemon mixture and spoon into the pastry case. Return to the oven and bake for about 40 minutes or until set and golden brown. Dust with icing sugar before serving.

COLD SOUFFLÉS

LEMON SOUFFLÉ

Serves 4

3 eggs, separated
175g, 6oz caster sugar
juice and grated rind of 2 lemons
15g, ½oz gelatine + 3 tbsp water
300ml, ½pt whipping cream

Whisk together the egg yolks, sugar, lemon rind and juice until thick and mousse-like. Dissolve the gelatine in the water and stir into the mixture. Whip the cream and fold it into the mousse. Lastly whisk the egg whites until fairly stiff and fold them in too. Turn into a serving bowl and chill to set.

BLACKCURRANT SOUFFLÉ

Serves 4 – 6

300ml, ½pt blackcurrant purée
4 eggs, separated
100g, 4oz caster sugar
juice of half a lemon
15g, ½oz gelatine + 4 tbsp water
150ml, ¼pt double cream, whipped

Beat the sugar, egg yolks, purée and lemon juice together in a mixing bowl until thick. Dissolve the gelatine in the water and pour over the egg and blackcurrant mixture in a thin stream, beating as you pour. Fold in the cream and lastly whisk the egg whites and fold them in too. Chill in the fridge and eat the same day.

HOT SOUFFLÉS

CHOCOLATE SOUFFLÉ

Serves 6 – 8

300ml, ½pt milk
15g, ½oz cornflour
1 tbsp espresso coffee
6 eggs, separated
100g, 4oz caster sugar
225g, 8oz dark chocolate, melted
icing sugar for dusting

Stir a spoonful of the milk into the cornflour and heat the rest with the coffee in a saucepan. Stir the cornflour mixture into the coffee-flavoured milk and keep stirring until the sauce boils. In a bowl whisk the egg yolks with the sugar until thick and beat in the melted chocolate. Stir in the coffee-flavoured milk. Lastly, whisk the egg whites until stiff and fold into the chocolate mixture using a metal spoon. Pour into a greased soufflé dish and bake in a pre heated oven at gas mark 6, 200°C (400°F) for 35 minutes. Serve immediately dusted with icing sugar.

LEMON AND LIME SOUFFLÉ

Serves 4 – 6

40g, 1½oz butter
40g, 1½oz plain flour
450ml, ¾pt milk
50g, 2oz caster sugar
grated rind of 1 small lemon and 1 lime
juice of ½ lemon
3 egg yolks + 4 egg whites

Melt the butter in a saucepan and add the flour. Gradually add the milk to make a roux and stir until smooth. Off the heat, stir in the sugar, lemon and lime rind and lemon juice. Beat in the egg yolks. Whisk the egg whites and fold them carefully in using a metal spoon. Turn into a greased soufflé dish and bake in a preheated oven at gas mark 5, 190°C (375°F) for about 25 minutes. Serve immediately dusted with icing sugar.

CHESTNUT SOUFFLÉ

Serves 6 - 8

1 large tin of sweetened chestnut purée
4 eggs, separated
1 tbsp brandy

Stir the egg yolks into the chestnut purée along with the brandy. Whisk the egg whites together until stiff and gently fold into the chestnut mixture. Transfer to a greased soufflé dish and cook in the oven at gas mark 6, 200°C (400°F) for 15 minutes. Serve immediately.

APPLE SOUFFLÉ OMELETTE

Serves 3 – 4

Filling

1 Cox's apple, peeled, cored and sliced
25g, 1oz butter
2 tbsp light brown sugar
3 tbsp single cream

4 eggs, separated
2 tbsp single cream
1 tbsp caster sugar
1 tbsp butter

For the filling, gently fry the slices of apple in the butter and sugar until tender. Stir in the cream and keep warm. To make the omelette beat the egg yolks with the cream and sugar. Whisk the egg whites and fold them in. Melt the butter in a frying pan and fry the omelette so that it browns underneath. Then place under a grill to brown the top. Add the apple filling and fold over. Dust with icing sugar and serve at once.

OTHER OVEN-BAKED PUDDINGS

PROFITEROLES WITH BUTTERSCOTCH SAUCE

Serves 6

Choux pastry
50g, 2oz butter
150ml, ¼pt water
60g, 2½oz plain flour, sifted
2 eggs, beaten

Filling
150ml, ¼pt whipping cream, whipped

Sauce
25g, 1oz butter
50g, 2oz dark brown sugar
150ml, ¼pt single cream

To make the profiteroles melt the butter in the water in a saucepan. Bring just to the boil and then add the flour all at once beating the flour until the mixture forms a ball. Cool slightly and then add the eggs a little at a time. Whisk the mixture until smooth and glossy. Put spoonfuls of this choux pastry on dampened baking sheets. Cook in a hot oven for 10 minutes and then lower the heat to gas mark 5, 190°C (375°F) and cook for a further 20 minutes until golden. Transfer to a rack to cool and slit each profiterole to let any air out. Fill with whipped cream. For the sauce, melt the butter and sugar and stir in the cream. Stir over a gentle heat until the sauce bubbles and becomes glossy. Pour over the profiteroles and serve.

CHOCOLATE ROULADE

Serves 6 – 8

For the roulade

175g, 6oz plain chocolate
6 eggs, separated
175g, 6oz sugar

Filling

300ml, ½pt double cream
1 tsp vanilla essence

Melt the chocolate either in a microwave or in a bowl over a pan of simmering water. Whisk the egg yolks with the sugar until thick and pale. Stir in the melted chocolate until smooth. Whisk the egg whites until stiff and using a metal spoon fold them into the chocolate mixture until well incorporated. Line a Swiss roll tin with baking parchment and pour the chocolate mixture into the tin, spreading it out evenly. Bake in a pre-heated oven at gas mark 4, 180°C (350°F) for 20 minutes until firm to the touch. Then remove from the oven, cover with a damp tea towel and leave for at least a couple of hours. Put another sheet of baking parchment on your work surface and sprinkle with icing or caster sugar. Tip the roulade out onto the baking parchment and tear off the bottom piece. Whip the double cream with the vanilla essence and spread over the roulade, before rolling up it like a Swiss roll. Dust with more icing sugar if necessary and serve at once. The roulade does not keep well.

LEMON ROULADE
WITH CHOCOLATE CREAM

Serves 8

For the roulade

5 eggs, separated
150g, 5oz caster sugar
grated rind and juice of 1 lemon
50g, 2oz ground almonds

For the filling

300ml, ½pt double cream
75g, 3oz dark chocolate, grated
50g, 2oz white chocolate, grated

Line a Swiss roll tin with greaseproof paper. To make the roulade, whisk the egg yolks in a bowl, gradually adding the caster sugar and whisking until the mixture is pale and thick. Whisk in the lemon juice and fold in the ground almonds and grated lemon rind. Whisk the egg whites until stiff and fold them into the lemon mixture. Pour into the Swiss roll tin. Bake in the oven at gas mark 4, 180°C (350°F) for about 20 minutes. Take out the roulade and cover with a damp tea towel. Leave for a few hours. To make the filling, whip the cream until thick but not too stiff. Fold in the grated chocolate. Place a piece of greaseproof paper on your work surface and cover with icing sugar. Tip the roulade out onto the icing sugar. Carefully peel off the lining paper. Spread the cream over the roulade and roll up. Don't worry if it splits in places. This is quite normal. Dust with more icing sugar before serving.

ICE CREAMS

All ice creams serve 6 - 8

VANILLA ICE CREAM

4 eggs, separated
100g, 4oz icing sugar
1 tsp vanilla essence
300ml, ½pt double cream

Whisk the egg yolks with half the icing sugar until thick and pale. Whisk the egg whites until stiff then gradually whisk in the remaining icing sugar a small amount at a time. Whisk the double cream with the vanilla essence until thick. Stir the cream into the egg yolk mixture and then fold in the egg whites. Make sure everything is thoroughly blended and then transfer to a freezer container. Freeze until firm.

MOLASSES ICE CREAM

A simple ice cream but much loved by my children.

3 eggs, separated
75g, 3oz molasses
50g, 2oz icing sugar
300ml, ½pt double cream

Whisk the egg yolks until thick and whisk in the molasses. Whisk the egg whites until stiff and whisk in the icing sugar. Whip the double cream. Fold the cream into the molasses mixture and then fold in the egg whites. Make sure everything is well incorporated and then transfer to a freezer container and freeze until firm.

GRANARY BREAD ICE CREAM

75g, 3oz granary bread, crusts removed
3 tbsp dark brown sugar
25g, 1oz melted butter
450ml, ¾pt double cream, lightly whipped
3 eggs, separated
1 tbsp honey + 1 tbsp brandy

Process the bread to form crumbs. Mix the brown sugar with the butter and add the crumbs. Spread this mixture on a baking sheet and bake for 15 minutes turning every so often until the crumbs are toasted. Beat the egg yolks, honey and brandy until thick. Whisk the egg whites and fold into the cream. Then fold this mixture into the egg yolks. Lastly mix in the breadcrumbs. Transfer to a freezer container and freeze until firm but remove from the freezer 15 minutes before you wish to serve it.

MAPLE SYRUP ICE CREAM

150ml, ¼pt maple syrup
3 eggs, separated
300ml, ½pt double cream
½ tsp vanilla essence

Heat the maple syrup until just below boiling point. Whisk the egg yolks together and whisk in some of the maple syrup. Stir this back into the hot syrup and cook over a gentle heat until the mixture thickens. Leave to cool. Whip the double cream with the vanilla essence and fold into the maple syrup mixture. Pour into a freezer container and freeze until just becoming firm. Then take out and beat well. Whisk the egg whites until stiff and fold them into the semi-frozen mixture. Freeze again until firm.

MOUSSES

CHOCOLATE POTS

Serves 6 – 8

175g, 6oz good plain chocolate
4 tbsp water
15g, ½oz butter
1 tsp vanilla essence
3 eggs, separated

Melt the chocolate with the water and butter and stir until smooth. Add the vanilla essence and stir in the egg yolks. Lastly whisk the egg whites until stiff and stir into the chocolate mixture. When all the egg white is well incorporated pour into ramekin dishes and chill overnight.

CHOCOLATE AND CRÈME FRAÎCHE MOUSSE

Serves 6 – 8

175g, 6oz plain chocolate
15g, ½oz butter
3 eggs, separated
1 x 200g, 8oz tub crème fraîche
white chocolate for decoration

Melt the chocolate and butter in the microwave or over a pan of simmering water. Stir the egg yolks into the melted chocolate mixture. Add the crème fraîche and stir until smooth. Whisk the egg whites until stiff and fold into the chocolate mixture. Pour into a serving bowl and chill until set. Decorate with shavings of white chocolate.

LEMON AND FROMAGE FRAIS MOUSSE

Serves 6

Juice and rind of 2 lemons + 1 tbsp water
15g, ½oz gelatine
3 eggs, separated
175g, 6oz caster sugar
225g, 8oz fromage frais

Mix half the lemon juice with the water and sprinkle the gelatine powder over the liquid, warming it until it dissolves. Beat the egg yolks with the lemon rind, rest of the lemon juice and 75g, 3oz of the caster sugar. Stir the gelatine into the egg yolk mixture. Whisk the egg whites until stiff and whisk in the remaining sugar. Fold the fromage frais into the mousse then fold in the egg whites. Transfer to a serving bowl and chill for a couple of hours.

LIME MOUSSE

Serves 4

3 eggs, separated
50g, 2oz caster sugar
grated rind and juice of 3 limes
15g, ½oz gelatine
300ml, ½pt double cream, whipped

Beat the egg yolks with the sugar until thick and creamy. Dissolve the gelatine in the lime juice over a pan of simmering water. Fold the egg yolk mixture into the whipped cream and then stir in the gelatine and the grated rind. Beat the egg whites until stiff and fold them into the mousse. Pour into a serving dish and leave to set in a cool place for a couple of hours.

CAKES

VICTORIA JAM SPONGE

175g, 6oz margarine
175g, 6oz caster sugar
3 eggs
175g, 6oz self-raising flour + 1 tbsp cornflour
2 tbsp milk
raspberry jam

Cream the butter and sugar together. Gradually beat in the eggs and the flour and milk. You can mix everything together in a food processor but add an extra teaspoon of baking powder to help the mixture rise in the oven. Divide the cake mixture between two 17.5cm, 7in greased cake tins and bake in the oven at gas mark 4 180°C (350°F) for 25 minutes. Turn out and sandwich together with raspberry jam.

CHOCOLATE MOUSSE CAKE

3 eggs
75g, 3oz sugar
150g, 5oz plain chocolate
50g, 2oz butter
1 tsp vanilla essence
25g, 1oz self-raising flour

Whisk the eggs and sugar together until thick. Melt the chocolate and butter together and stir in the vanilla essence. Mix the melted chocolate into the eggs and sugar. Sift the flour over the mixture and fold it in. Pour into a greased 20cm, 8in cake tin and bake in a preheated oven at gas mark 5, 190°C (375°F) for 25 minutes. Allow to cool before turning out. This should be served as a pudding with cream.

LIGHT LEMON SPONGE

This is one of my favourite cakes.

100g, 4oz caster sugar
3 eggs, separated
1 tbsp lemon juice
75g, 3oz plain flour
½ tsp baking powder

Filling

50g, 2oz butter
100g, 4oz icing sugar
¼ tsp grated lemon zest
1 tsp lemon juice

Icing

100g, 4 oz icing sugar
2 tbsp lemon juice

Beat together the egg yolks and sugar until light and creamy. Stir in the lemon juice. Sift the flour and fold carefully into the egg and sugar mixture. Beat the egg whites until fairly stiff and fold them in as well. Divide the mixture between two 17.5cm, 7in greased cake tins, lined with baking parchment. Bake in the oven at gas mark 4, 180°C (350°F) for 15 minutes. Remove and allow to cool on a wire rack. To make the filling beat the butter and gradually beat in the icing sugar. Add the lemon zest and juice and beat again. Use this butter cream to sandwich the two cakes together. Mix the lemon juice with the icing sugar and pour this over the cake. Leave to set. This cake is best eaten the day it is made or at least by the next day.

WHISKED CHOCOLATE SPONGE

For an alternative filling try the meringue butter cream on page 133 but halve the recipe to fill this sponge and add the teaspoon of cocoa powder when creaming the butter.

3 eggs, separated
100g, 4oz caster sugar
1 tbsp warm water
50g, 2oz self-raising flour
15g, ½oz cornflour
15g, ½oz cocoa powder

Filling

50g, 2oz butter
100g, 4oz icing sugar
1 tsp drinking chocolate
1 tsp single cream
few drops of vanilla essence
icing sugar for dusting

Whisk the egg yolks with the caster sugar until thick and creamy. Stir in the tablespoon of warm water. Sieve the flour, baking powder and cocoa over the egg mixture and fold it in until well incorporated. Whisk the egg whites until stiff and fold them in. Divide the mixture between two well greased 17.5cm, 7in cake tins and bake in the oven at gas mark 4, 180°C (350°F) for 20 minutes. To make the filling beat the icing sugar into the butter, add the drinking chocolate, cream and vanilla essence and beat well together. Use this mixture to sandwich the cakes together. Dust with icing sugar if liked.

WHITE CHOCOLATE SPONGE
WITH RASPBERRIES AND CREAM

4 eggs
100g, 4oz caster sugar
100g, 4oz plain flour
75g 3oz white chocolate, grated

Filling

100g, 4oz raspberries
150ml, ¼pt double cream

Whisk the eggs with the caster sugar until pale and thick. Sift the flour over the egg mixture and add the chocolate. Fold carefully together making sure everything is well incorporated. Turn into two 20cm, 8in greased cake tins and bake in a preheated oven at gas mark 4, 180°C (350°F) for 20 minutes. Meanwhile whip the cream and fold in the raspberries. Turn out the cakes, cool on a wire rack and sandwich together with the raspberries and cream.

SWISS ROLLS

CHOCOLATE SWISS ROLL

For an alternative filling try the meringue butter cream on page 133.

3 eggs
100g, 4oz caster sugar
1 tbsp hot water
50g, 2oz plain flour
25g, 1oz cocoa powder

Filling

150ml, ¼pt double cream
50g, 2oz icing sugar
½ tsp vanilla essence
icing sugar for dusting

Whisk together the eggs and caster sugar until pale and thick. Stir in the hot water. Sieve the flour and cocoa powder over the egg mixture and fold it in quickly but carefully. Turn into a lined and greased Swiss roll tin and bake in the oven at gas mark 6, 200°C (400°F) for 10 minutes. Dampen a tea towel with hot water and lay out on the work surface. Lay a piece of greaseproof paper over the tea towel and sprinkle caster sugar over it. Turn the Swiss roll out onto the greaseproof paper and carefully roll up with the lining paper inside. Allow to cool while you whip the cream with the icing sugar and vanilla essence. Unroll and spread the cream over the chocolate sponge before rolling up again. Sprinkle with icing sugar before serving.

JAM SWISS ROLL

This is a slightly different way of making a Swiss roll than in the more traditional recipe used in the chocolate Swiss roll. I think this method is less likely to crack when rolled up.

3 eggs, separated
75g, 3oz icing sugar
75g, 3oz self-raising flour, sifted

Filling

4 tbsp raspberry jam
150ml, ¼pt double cream, whipped

Whisk the egg yolks with half the icing sugar until pale and thick. Fold the flour into the egg yolk mixture. Whisk the egg whites until they stand in peaks and whisk in the remaining icing sugar. Fold the egg whites into the egg yolk mixture. Turn into a lined and greased Swiss roll tin and bake in the oven at gas mark 5, 190°C (375°F) for 12 minutes. Lay a tea towel on your work surface and sprinkle with icing sugar. Turn the Swiss roll out onto the tea towel and peel off the lining paper. Roll up with the tea towel inside and allow to cool for a few minutes. Unroll and spread with raspberry jam and the cream before rolling up again. Allow to rest for an hour before slicing.

COFFEE AND WALNUT SWISS ROLL

3 eggs
75g, 3oz caster sugar
75g, 3oz self-raising flour
1 tbsp coffee essence
50g, 2oz walnuts, ground

Filling

150ml, ¼pt double cream
25g, 1oz icing sugar
1 tbsp coffee essence

Whisk together the eggs and caster sugar until pale and thick. Sieve the flour over the egg mixture and fold it in along with the coffee essence and walnuts quickly but carefully. Turn into a lined and greased Swiss roll tin and bake in the oven at gas mark 6, 200°C (400°F) for 10 minutes. Dampen a tea towel with hot water and lay out on the work surface. Lay a piece of greaseproof paper over the tea towel and sprinkle caster sugar over it. Turn the Swiss roll out onto the greaseproof paper and carefully roll up with the lining paper inside. Allow to cool while you whip the cream with the icing sugar and coffee essence. Unroll and spread the coffee cream over the walnut sponge before rolling up again. Sprinkle with icing sugar before serving.

LEMON SWISS ROLL WITH LEMON CURD

3 eggs
100g, 4oz sugar
1 tbsp lemon juice
75g, 3oz plain flour

Filling
3 tbsp lemon curd
150ml, ¼pt double cream

Whisk together the eggs and caster sugar until pale and thick. Stir in the lemon juice. Sieve the flour over the egg mixture and fold in quickly but carefully. Turn into a lined and greased Swiss roll tin and bake in the oven at gas mark 6, 200°C (400°F) for 10 minutes. Turn out the Swiss roll as in the previous recipe. Whip up the cream with the lemon curd. Unroll and spread with the lemon curd mixture before rolling up again. Dust with icing sugar.

LEMON CURD

Makes 450g, 1lb

2 eggs
1 tsp custard powder
150g, 5oz caster sugar
50g, 2oz butter
grated rind and juice of 2 lemons

In a mixing bowl beat the eggs with the custard powder and add the sugar, butter, lemon rind and juice. Put this bowl over a pan of simmering water and stir the mixture from time to time until it thickens. Leave to cool and pour into jars.

RECIPES USING EGG YOLKS

CHICKEN AND LEMON SOUP

Serves 6

25g, 1oz butter
1 onion, peeled and chopped
1.2 litres, 2pt chicken stock
100g, 4oz cooked chicken meat, chopped
1 tbsp cornflour
3 tbsp lemon juice
salt and pepper
150ml, ¼pt double cream
2 egg yolks
1 tbsp chopped fresh chives

Melt the butter in a large saucepan and gently cook the onion. Place the onion, stock and cooked chicken in a food processor and add the cornflour. Process for a couple of minutes and then return to the pan and bring to the boil. Stir in the lemon juice, salt and pepper. Lastly, add the cream and cook slightly. Mix a little soup with the egg yolks and then add to the pan but do not allow to boil. Serve immediately with chopped chives.

SPINACH QUICHE

Serves 4 – 6

175g, 6oz shortcrust pastry

For the filling

225g, 8oz spinach
15g, ½oz butter
300ml, ½pt single cream
4 egg yolks
100g, 4oz cream cheese

Roll out the pastry and use to line a greased 20cm, 8in flan dish. Prick the base and bake blind for 10 minutes in the oven at gas mark 4, 180°C (350°F). Cook the spinach in a covered saucepan with the butter for several minutes. Chop finely and use to cover the base of the pastry case. Beat together the cream, egg yolks and cream cheese and pour over the spinach. Cook in the oven at gas mark 5, 190°C (375°F) for 30 minutes.

CRÈME BRULÉE

Serves 6

4 egg yolks
50g, 2oz caster sugar
1 tsp vanilla essence
600ml, 1pt single cream
50g, 2oz demerara sugar

Beat the egg yolks with the sugar and beat in the vanilla essence. Heat the cream over a pan of simmering water until just below boiling point. Stir into the egg yolk mixture and strain into 6 greased ramekin dishes. Place the ramekins into a roasting tin half filled with water and bake in the oven at gas mark 4, 180°C (350°F) for about 25 minutes until just set. Leave to cool. Sprinkle demerara sugar over the top of each ramekin and put under the grill to caramelise or use a blow torch. Chill for about two hours before serving. Don't chill for too long or the caramel topping will go soft.

ZABAGLIONE

Serves 4

4 egg yolks
75g, 3oz caster sugar
120ml, 4fl oz Marsala

Put the egg yolks and sugar in a bowl and beat over a saucepan of simmering water until very pale and thick. Then gradually add the Marsala, a tablespoon at a time while you continue to whisk. You will need to whisk for about 20 minutes. You must add the Marsala slowly and allow the mixture to thicken or it will separate. Pour into 4 glasses and serve.

CREME CARAMEL

Serves 4

175g, 6oz granulated sugar
150ml, ¼pt water
2 egg yolks + 3 eggs
50g, 2oz caster sugar
1 tsp vanilla essence
600ml, 1pt milk

Combine the water and granulated sugar in a saucepan and heat gently until the sugar has dissolved. Bring to the boil and cook without stirring until the mixture is golden brown. Pour into the bottom of a 600ml, 1pt mould or into six individual ramekin dishes. Beat the egg yolks, whole eggs, caster sugar and vanilla essence together. Warm the milk and stir into the egg mixture. Strain and pour on to the sugar syrup. Fill a roasting tin half full with water and place the mould or ramekin dishes in the tin. Bake in the oven at gas mark 3, 160°C (325°F) for 1 hour and 10 minutes (40 minutes if using ramekins) or until set. Cool and then chill for a few hours before serving.

MOUSSEY BUTTER CREAM FILLING

150ml, ¼pt single cream
2 egg yolks
½ tsp flour
50g, 2oz butter
50g, 2oz icing sugar
½ tsp vanilla essence

Whisk together the cream, egg yolks and flour in a bowl over a pan of simmering water until thick. Cream together the butter and icing sugar and gradually beat into the cooled egg yolk mixture. Use to fill a cake.

LEMON RICE PUDDING

Serves 4 – 6

600ml, 1pt milk
50g, 2oz pudding rice
large piece of lemon rind
50g, 2oz caster sugar
2 egg yolks
1 tsp lemon juice

Put the rice into an ovenproof dish along with the caster sugar and lemon rind. Pour over the milk. Cook for 2 hours in the oven at gas mark 2, 140°C (300°F) until creamy. Add a little more milk if the pudding becomes too dry. Beat the egg yolks with the lemon juice. Add a little of the hot milk from the rice, then stir the mixture into the creamed rice. Return to the oven for a further 20 minutes. Remove the lemon rind and serve with cream or crème fraîche.

WHITE CHOCOLATE HEAVENS

Serves 5

These are little white chocolate ice creams frozen in ramekins.

75g, 3oz white chocolate +1 tbsp single cream
3 egg yolks
50g, 2oz caster sugar
210ml, 7fl oz double cream

Melt the white chocolate in the microwave or over a pan of simmering water. Stir in the single cream – this will help give a smooth texture. Whisk the egg yolks and sugar together until thick and creamy. Then fold in the melted white chocolate, followed by the double cream. Pour into 5 ramekin dishes and freeze.

TREACLE TART ICE CREAM

Serves 6 - 8

50g, 2oz brown breadcrumbs
40g, 1½oz melted butter
6 egg yolks
150ml, ¼pt golden syrup, warmed
1 tbsp lemon juice
300ml, ½pt whipping cream, whipped

Mix together the breadcrumbs and melted butter. Put under the grill for a few minutes laid out on a baking sheet to crisp. Whisk the egg yolks until thick and pour the golden syrup in a steady stream onto the yolks as you whisk them. Whisk in the lemon juice. Stir in the whipped cream and fold in the cooled breadcrumbs. Turn into a freezer container and freeze until firm.

RICH LEMON ICE CREAM

This is a quick and easy ice cream to make and needs no extra beating once put in the freezer.

Serves 8

225g, 8oz caster sugar
8 egg yolks
grated rind of 2 large lemons
4 tbsp lemon juice
300ml, ½pt double cream

Warm the sugar in either the oven or a microwave (this quickens the whisking process). Put the egg yolks in a mixing bowl and add the caster sugar. Whisk until very thick and whisk in the lemon rind. Whisk the cream and lemon juice together and fold into the egg yolk mixture. Turn into a freezer container and freeze until firm. Remove 15 minutes before you wish to serve the ice cream.

PEAR ICE CREAM

This delicious ice cream would go well with a compôte of red berries.

Serves 4 – 6

450g, 1lb pears, peeled, cored and sliced
50g, 2oz butter
50g, 2oz sugar
1 tbsp elderflower syrup
strip of lemon peel
3 egg yolks
150ml, ¼pt crème fraîche
150ml, ¼pt double cream

Cook the pear slices gently with the butter, sugar, elderflower syrup, lemon peel and 4 tablespoons of water in a saucepan, until soft. Remove the peel and purée the fruit. Beat in the egg yolks and cook over a low heat until the mixture thickens, stirring constantly. Leave to cool, stirring every so often. Pour the mixture into a container and freeze for about an hour. Whip the crème fraîche and cream together and fold into the half frozen pear mixture. Cover and freeze until firm.

RASPBERRY ICE CREAM

Serves 6 – 8

450g, 1lb raspberries, puréed and sieved
2 tbsp icing sugar
squeeze of lemon juice
120ml, 4fl oz water
75g, 3oz granulated sugar
3 egg yolks
300ml, ½pt double cream

Add the icing sugar and lemon juice to the sieved raspberries. Dissolve the sugar in the water and then bring to the boil and keep it boiling for a couple of minutes. Meanwhile whisk the egg yolks until pale and thick and then slowly whisk in the sugar syrup in a steady stream. Continue to whisk the mixture as it cools. Fold the egg yolk mixture into the raspberry purée. Whip the cream and fold that in too. Stir until the mixture is smooth. Pour into a freezer container and freeze until firm.

MASCARPONE ICE CREAM

Serves 6

2 egg yolks
50g, 2oz icing sugar
225g, 8oz mascarpone
2 tsp vanilla essence

Whisk together the egg yolks and icing sugar until really thick. Beat the mascarpone and vanilla essence into the egg yolk mixture. Transfer to a freezer container and freeze until firm.

BUTTERSCOTCH AND WALNUT TART

Serves 6 - 8

Shortcrust pastry made with 175g, 6oz flour and 75g, 3oz margarine

200g, 7oz dark muscovado sugar
240ml, 8 floz single cream
75g, 3oz butter
50g, 2oz cornflour, sifted
3 egg yolks
1 tsp vanilla essence
100g, 4oz walnuts

Roll out the pastry and use to line a greased 23cm, 9in flan dish. Bake the pastry case blind in the oven at gas mark 5, 190°C (375°F) for 15 minutes. Put the sugar, cream, butter, cornflour, egg yolks and vanilla essence in a bowl and whisk until thick and creamy. Pour into the pastry case and sprinkle the walnuts over the butterscotch. Bake in the oven at gas mark 4, 180°C (350°F) for 20 minutes. Serve warm with crème fraîche or Greek yoghurt.

FRENCH APPLE FLAN

Serves 6 – 8

Sweet pastry (see page 93)

Custard

100g, 4oz caster sugar
3 tbsp cornflour
½ tsp vanilla essence
450ml, ¾pt milk
4 egg yolks

Topping

700g, 1½lb cooking apples, peeled, cored and sliced
50g, 2oz butter
50g, 2oz demerara sugar

Roll out the pastry and use to line a greased 23cm, 9in flan dish. Chill for 30 minutes and then prick and bake blind in the oven at gas mark 5, 190°C (375°F) for 20 minutes. Make the custard by putting the sugar in a saucepan with the cornflour and vanilla essence and blend with a little milk. Add the rest of the milk and bring to the boil, stirring all the time until the mixture thickens. Remove from the heat and beat in the egg yolks one at a time. Return to the heat and cook gently for 5 minutes, stirring all the time. Do not boil. Turn off the heat and allow to cool before pouring into the pastry shell. Slice the apples and fry in the butter, sprinkled with the sugar. When almost tender arrange on top of the custard in overlapping layers. Serve warm or cold.

126

MAYONNAISE

2 egg yolks
1 tsp mustard powder
1 tsp sugar
salt and black pepper
150ml, ¼pt olive oil
150ml, ¼pt sunflower oil
3 tbsp white wine vinegar

Put the egg yolks, mustard powder, sugar and seasoning in a food processor and whiz for a few seconds. Start adding the oil, drip by drip and then in a slow steady trickle. Do not add it too fast or the mixture will curdle. When you have added about half of the oils you can add the vinegar tablespoon by tablespoon. Then add the rest of the oil in the same way as before. If the mixture curdles you can rescue it by adding another egg yolk. Beat the extra yolk and then add the curdled mayonnaise to it very slowly, beating all the time. This should give you a smooth mayonnaise.

VANILLA CUSTARD

2 egg yolks
1 tbsp sugar
300ml, ½pt full fat milk
1 tsp vanilla essence or ½ vanilla pod, split

Whisk the egg yolks. Put the sugar, milk and essence or vanilla pod together in a saucepan and bring slowly to the boil. Remove the pod if using and pour the milk onto the egg yolks. Return to the pan and stir over a gentle heat until the liquid thickens. Serve hot or cold.

LIME CUSTARD

Grated rind of 2 limes
450ml, ¾pt milk
4 egg yolks
50g, 2oz caster sugar

Put the lime peel in the milk and bring to the boil. Simmer the milk for 5 minutes. Beat the egg yolks with the sugar until very thick and gradually pour on the milk in a thin stream, stirring all the time. Heat gently until the custard begins to thicken. Strain through a fine sieve and serve hot or cold.

HOLLANDAISE SAUCE

2 egg yolks
1 tsp white wine vinegar
75g, 3oz hot melted butter

Whiz the egg yolks in a blender or small food processor with the teaspoon of white wine vinegar. Pour the melted butter gradually onto the egg yolks with the motor still running. The sauce will thicken. Serve immediately.

SABAYON SAUCE

3 egg yolks
75g, 3oz caster sugar
1 glass of white wine or sherry

Beat the yolks with the sugar until very thick and pale in a bowl over a pan of simmering water. Add the wine and continue to whisk until the sauce is thick. Serve at once poured over raspberries or other summer fruits.

RECIPES USING EGG WHITES

ALL SORTS OF MERINGUES

All meringues should be prepared in a very clean dry bowl to enable the maximum amount of air to be incorporated when you whisk them. Any water, grease or egg yolk that gets in with the whites will prevent them from obtaining this volume of air. Always use a metal spoon when folding in sugar or other flavourings. Four egg whites will make about 20 small meringues, 3 egg whites about 15.

TRADITIONAL MERINGUES

4 egg whites
225g, 8oz caster sugar

Whisk the egg whites until stiff enough to hold a peak or remain in the bowl when reversed. It is very important that the egg whites are stiff before you add the sugar. Whisk in half the caster sugar and then fold in the rest. You should now have a stiff meringue mixture which you can put in small spoonfuls onto greased baking sheets. Place the meringues in the oven at gas mark 1, 130°C (275°F). If you like meringues that are soft in the centre they will be ready in about an hour and a half. Otherwise reduce the oven slightly and leave for another half hour – these meringues will have a chewy centre. If you want meringues that are crunchy all the way through leave to cook for at least another half hour at the slightly lower temperature, so that they will have had two and a half hours altogether. Then switch off the oven and leave to cool inside for another 20 minutes.

BROWN SUGAR MERINGUES

4 egg whites
100g, 4oz caster sugar
100g, 4oz light soft brown sugar

Whisk the egg whites until stiff. Mix together the two sugars and while you continue to whisk the egg whites, whisk in a tablespoon of sugar at a time until all is incorporated. The meringue should be very stiff. Put spoonfuls onto greased baking sheets and warm the oven. Cook the meringues for 20 minutes at gas mark 1, 130°C (275°F) and then reduce to gas mark ½ 120°C (250°F) and cook for another 2 hours. Leave in the oven until completely cold.

MUSCOVADO MERINGUES

3 egg whites
175g, 6oz light or dark muscovado sugar

Sieve the muscovado sugar to get rid of any lumps. Whisk the egg whites until very stiff and then whisk in the muscovado sugar a tablespoon at a time being very careful to make sure each tablespoon is incorporated before you add the next. Put spoonfuls of meringue onto greased baking sheets and cook as above.

CHOCOLATE MERINGUES

These meringues made with icing sugar are a slightly different type called Meringue Cuite. Used mostly for meringue baskets and for piping they make a firmer, denser sort of meringue.

4 egg whites
225g, 8oz icing sugar
25g, 1oz cocoa powder
few drops of vanilla essence

Whisk the egg whites with the icing sugar in a bowl over a pan of simmering water for several minutes until very thick. Then take the bowl off the heat and sieve the cocoa powder over the meringue mixture and, using a metal spoon, fold it gently in along with the vanilla essence. Spoon or pipe the meringues onto greased baking sheets and bake in a very low oven for 3 hours.

MERINGUE ITALIENNE

3 egg whites
225g, 8oz granulated sugar
3 tbsp water
few drops of vanilla essence

Put the water and sugar in a saucepan and heat gently until the sugar dissolves. Then boil rapidly until the temperature reaches 150°C (300°F) on a sugar thermometer or until a small amount dropped into cold water forms a hard ball. Whisk the egg whites until stiff and pour on the hot syrup in a steady stream while you continue to whisk and add the vanilla essence. This meringue can be used in cake fillings, for a trifle topping or instead of whipped cream.

HAZELNUT MERINGUE CAKE

This is a meringue cake with two layers sandwiched together.

4 egg whites
225g, 8oz caster sugar
1 tsp white wine vinegar
1 tsp vanilla essence
100g, 4oz ground hazelnuts

Filling

210ml, 7fl oz double cream, whipped
100g, 4oz raspberries

Whisk the egg whites until very stiff. Whisk in the sugar, a tablespoon at a time until all is incorporated. Add the vinegar and vanilla essence and fold in the ground hazelnuts using a metal spoon. Grease two baking sheets and divide the meringue into two equal circles about 20cm, 8in in diameter on the sheets. Cook in the oven at gas mark 4, 180°C (350°F) for about 35 minutes. The meringue circles may crack and crumble a little when you turn them out. Fold the raspberries into the cream and sandwich between the layers of meringue.

COFFEE MERINGUE BISCUITS

2 egg whites
100g, 4oz caster sugar
100g, 4oz ground almonds

Filling

1 tsp instant coffee
1 tsp hot water
25g, 1oz butter
50g, 2oz icing sugar

Whisk the egg whites until they are stiff and then fold in the sugar and ground almonds. Place small spoonfuls of this mixture on to the baking sheet and bake in the oven at gas mark 5, 190°C (375°F) for 10 minutes or until the biscuits turn pale brown. Cool on a wire rack. Make the filling by dissolving the coffee in the teaspoon of water and beat this into the butter and icing sugar. Use this mixture to sandwich the biscuits together.

MERINGUE BUTTER CREAM

A useful way of using up 2 egg whites for filling a cake. The mixture looks like clotted cream but is not so calorific!

2 egg whites
100g, 4oz icing sugar
100g, 4oz butter, creamed

Whisk together the egg whites and icing sugar in a bowl over a pan of simmering water until really thick. Gradually beat the meringue into the creamed butter. You could add a flavouring of a teaspoon of cocoa powder to the butter or grated lemon rind, vanilla or coffee essence.

MONT BLANC

Makes 4-5 Meringue Nests

3 egg whites
175g, 6oz caster sugar
1 large tin of sweetened chestnut purée
300ml, ½pt whipping cream
cocoa powder for dusting

Make the meringue mixture as in Traditional Meringues on page 129. Put large spoonfuls on a greased baking sheet and flatten in the middle to form nests. Bake in the oven at gas mark 1, 120°C (275°F) for about an hour and a half, then switch off the oven and allow to cool completely. Transfer the meringue nests to a serving dish. Whip the cream and fold half into the chestnut purée. Divide between the meringue nests and add an extra dollop of cream on top of each one. Serve immediately dusted with a little cocoa powder if liked.

APPLE MERINGUE

Serves 4 - 6

4 large Bramley apples, peeled, cored and sliced
a little butter
2 tbsp apricot jam
grated rind and juice of 1 lemon
100g, 4oz brown sugar
3 eating apples, peeled, cored and quartered
100g, 4oz granulated sugar + 2tbsp water

Meringue

2 egg whites
100g, 4oz caster sugar
25g, 1oz ground almonds
icing sugar

Cook the sliced Bramley apples with the butter, jam, lemon rind, juice and brown sugar until soft. Beat to a purée. Cool slightly and spread over the base of a round pie dish. Poach the eating apples in a syrup made from the granulated sugar and water. Do not allow them to break up. Drain and arrange on top of the apple purée. Whip the whites until stiff and gradually beat in the sugar. Stir in the ground almonds. Spread the meringue mixture over the apple, sprinkle with a little icing sugar and cook in the oven at gas mark 4, 180°C (350°F) for 30 minutes.

PEAR AND RASPBERRY PAVLOVA

For the Pavlova

4 egg whites
225g, 8oz caster sugar
½ tbsp cornflour, sifted
1 tsp vinegar
1 tsp vanilla essence

150ml, ¼pt whipping cream
150ml, ¼pt soured cream
225g, 8oz pears, peeled, cored and sliced
225g, 8oz raspberries
50g, 2oz sugar

To make the Pavlova beat the egg whites until stiff. Gradually beat in the sugar, a little at a time. Sprinkle the cornflour, vinegar and vanilla over the mixture and fold in carefully. Make a circle with the meringue mixture on a large greased baking sheet. Bake for an hour at gas mark 1, 120°C (275°F). The Pavlova should be crisp on the outside with a soft marshmallow centre. Whip the cream with the soured cream. Spread this over the meringue. Cook the raspberries with the sugar over a gentle heat until the juices run. Add the pears and cook for a couple more minutes. Carefully pour the pear slices and raspberries over the cream and serve at once.

STRAWBERRY SNOW

Serves 4 – 6

450g, 1lb strawberries
75g, 3oz caster sugar
a few drops of vanilla essence
3 egg whites
150ml, ¼pt double cream, whipped

Purée and sieve the strawberries. Stir in the sugar and vanilla essence. Beat the egg whites until stiff and fold then into the purée along with the whipped cream.

RASPBERRY AND REDCURRANT MOUSSE

Serves 4 – 6

225g, 8oz raspberries
225g, 8oz redcurrants
150g, 5oz sugar
2 egg whites

Sieve the raspberries and redcurrants to remove all pips. Add the sugar. Whisk the egg whites until stiff and fold into the purée. In a saucepan over a low heat, whisk the mixture for about 3 minutes until the mixture thickens and starts to rise. Pour into glasses or a serving bowl and leave to cool before serving. If left for a while some of the juice will separate and sink to the bottom but can be whipped up again before serving.

AVOCADO AND LIME WHIP

This is an unusual combination of ingredients but delicious all the same.

2 ripe avocados
juice of 1 lime
6 tbsp single cream
2 egg whites
50g, 2oz icing sugar, sifted

Purée the avocados with the lime juice and single cream in a food processor. Whisk the egg whites until stiff and whisk in the icing sugar, a little at a time. Carefully fold in the avocado mixture and spoon into individual glasses or into one serving bowl. Serve straightaway.

BLACKCURRANT AND LIME SORBET

300ml, ½pt water
150g, 5oz granulated sugar
juice of 1 lime
450g, 1lb blackcurrants
2 egg whites

Put the water and sugar in a saucepan and heat gently until the sugar has dissolved. Bring to the boil and boil for 5 minutes until syrupy. Remove from the heat, stir in the lime juice and leave to cool. Meanwhile put the blackcurrants in a saucepan and heat gently until the juices start to run which should be after about 5 minutes. Sieve the blackcurrants and stir the blackcurrant purée into the cooled syrup. Freeze for an hour and then remove the slushy blackcurrant mixture and beat thoroughly. Whisk the egg whites until stiff and fold these into the blackcurrant mixture. Freeze until firm.

SECTION THREE

A COLLECTION OF ANECDOTES

SURROGATE MUMS
by JOSEPHINE PULLEIN-THOMPSON

I bought a pair of Silkies, beautiful fluffy white birds with blue skins and feathered legs. The hen had an elegant blue face and a puff of soft white feathers on her head; the cock's face was apoplectically purple and his crest composed of stiffer feathers. I named them Hero and Star and loved them dearly. I wrote a very bad poem to them, beginning 'Oh Hero and Star, how lovely you are …' Diana had bought Frizzles and Christine Japanese bantams. We set them up with houses; I painted mine yellow and bought yellow dishes to match. Christine's house and dishes were blue, Diana's green. The bantams wore rings in our colours, except for the Silkies whose legs were too feathered.

Our father began to take an interest and, despising the collection of mongrel chickens which roamed the yard and orchard, he bought some pure-bred hens – White Wyandottes and Rhode Island Reds – from a golfing friend. As with all his schemes, financial expenditure was necessary: a new hen house, with divided sleeping quarters and two runs, was set up against the orchard and top meadow hedge. I found myself in charge, which was quite demanding as they had to be fed and watered separately from all the other chickens.

A later purchase was an incubator. This was housed in the spare bedroom, the one tidy room in the house; it never recovered.

Fascinated by procreation, I cheerfully carried out the small chores of turning and damping the eggs and, like an intervening midwife, assisting the arrival of the chicks by picking at the outside of the shells once they were pipped from within. I would watch over the chicks as they dried off and then take them out to the brooder, where they spent their motherless infancy.

My mother's acquisition of guinea-fowl – in Oxfordshire they were known as gleanies – was as usual more romantic and less demanding of outlay. Wild and scorning chicken houses, the gleanies roosted in one of the taller apple trees. They laid their eggs, brown, pointed, and slightly smaller than hens' eggs, in communal nests, generally in patches of stinging nettles; with shells so hard that they survived falling from a height, they were perfect for mounted egg-and-spoon races.

We had become indifferent to nettle stings, rarely needing the antidote of a dock leaf, and when eggs ran out we would be sent to search for the gleanie nest. Our largest find was 80 eggs, all reasonably fresh.

The guinea-fowl hens were deplorable mothers. Frequently two of them would sit on one nest and appear with about 20 of the tiny chicks – grey and mouse-like with orange legs. Then they trailed them round in the tall, wet grass until they died from exhaustion. We tried shutting them in runs, but the hens, frantic at captivity, would dash themselves against the wire netting and trample on the chicks. Setting the eggs under bantams seemed the only solution and the grown chicks appeared to have no problems in recognising themselves as guinea-fowl; they would join the flock and roost in the apple tree as soon as they could fly.

*An extract from **Fair Girls and Grey Horses – Memories of a country childhood** by Josephine, Diana and Christine Pullein-Thompson published by Allison & Busby, 1996.*

BANTAMS AND KITTENS,
MEMORIES from MY MOTHER

When we were young, our granary was full of hay and straw and much in demand for maternity purposes – cats produced kittens there, bantams hatched chicks. Then twice in the same week something extraordinary happened. A cat left her mewing kittens to go hunting and almost at once, a bantam, deserting her eggs, went to cover the cold kittens with her wings. It seemed even more extraordinary, when this happened a second time and another bantam repeated the exercise, taking her newly hatched chicks with her. I must add that our poultry and cats got on extremely well together – no chicks were ever killed by our cats.

USES FOR EGGS
from PLEASURABLE POULTRY KEEPING
by EDWARD BROWN (1893)

The yolks of eggs, made into a paste with honey and flour, of about the consistency of mustard, gives speedy relief to one afflicted with boils. The white used as a coating for scalds and burns excludes the air, which so aggravates the sufferings of a burned person ... The white beaten with sugar is invaluable in bronchial infections, especially in hoarseness, when a little lemon juice may be added with good results. Leather chair seats may be revived by rubbing them well with beaten whites of eggs. Leather binding of books may also be cleaned by this method.

BOB'S BANTAM MEMORIES
by BOB WALKER BROWN

Some years ago I found, as a fly fisherman, that it was increasingly difficult to obtain good quality cocks' hackles for dry (floating) flies. A good quality hackle comes from a bird of at least three, preferably four, years of age. Commercially cocks are killed as soon as they are fit for the table and the neck hackles (cape) from such birds are too soft to be effective. Seeing an advertisement in the local paper for two pairs of bantams, I had one of my frequent brilliant ideas (or as my wife thought, quite the reverse). The two young cocks and two hens were owned by a boy of about 12 who treated them as pets until his mother got tired of their presence in her kitchen and made him switch to rabbits.

Driving home minus a cage, oncoming drivers gaped at the sight of one cock perched on my bald head, which it used as a loo, and the other on my shoulder. Arriving home I proudly placed all four birds on the kitchen table and called my wife. "Oh dear, what have you done?" she said before two birds immediately decorated a shoulder and her newly permed hair.

All four birds transferred their attachment from the small boy to me and followed me everywhere until my two Springer Spaniels thought this was too much. Housed in an old stable the bantams thrived and I hoped that in a few years I would have a walking/flying source of magnificent cock hackles, to be gently plucked a few at a time.

In the course of the next year the birds multiplied at a phenomenal rate; the new young cocks seemed to have but one aim: to murder all other young cocks. Some were so badly injured that they had to be killed, rather than increasing my dream of endless hackles.

Some 18 months later, the garden was overrun with bantams who occasionally took to their wings and had to be rounded up from nearby neighbours' gardens. "Oh well," I thought, "at least there are the eggs." But I was working in London and our two Springers usually found the eggs, laid in thick ground cover, before my wife. It became increasingly clear that my wife did not think much of me as a bantam-fancier, especially when, after covering rows of vegetable seedlings with yards of plastic cloche, carefully closing the ends, we returned from Spain to find that the plastic cloches had merely served to cover the birds as they decimated all the seedlings. In between raiding the vegetable garden the bantams had scratched their way round the edges of all the flower beds, throwing up bits of stone just the right size to wreck the lawn mower.

The end came when my wife found eight bantams decorating her kitchen table and others strutting in the hall. I was sorry to part with such amusing creatures and gave some 34 away to a keen bantam man; I also gave him 20 eggs of uncertain age and of that number no less than 16 hatched. I then had to buy American hackles at £60!

KILLER IN OUR MIDST by ALISTAIR FYFE

They arrived courtesy of the postman. The small cardboard box was battered at one corner but its precious contents were intact. The ten bantam eggs, a combination of silver, gold, and blue-laced Wyandotte were to join our flock of 12 Heinz 57s and form the basis of a select pedigree breed we could develop and sell on. Tilly was sitting, and had been, for about a week, on three crock eggs. She had already been a Mum twice. She was our best Mother, reliable, diligent, caring and tough on the others who showed too much interest in her chicks. Lifting Tilly gently and suffering an initial blizzard of pecks she settled in my arms while the eggs were exchanged. The three became ten and, as she was lowered back onto the nest, she was unfussed and using her beak she arranged them and, with a wiggle of her tail, she settled back to her duty, resigned to her long still hours on the nest.

Some 20 days later, expecting good news, sure enough the cheeping from beneath Tilly indicated she was a Mum again. Left for a few hours we returned in the evening to count six chicks with the possibility of more in the morning. After a chilly night we returned to see how Tilly was doing. The chicks, which were now exploring, rushed for sanctuary beneath her warm body as we opened the hen house door. She was becoming restless on the eggs and it was difficult to count how many chicks we had. Another day and Tilly had all but left the nest. We had a proud Mum, eight chicks and two eggs unhatched that we then removed.

With her clutch surrounding her, the chicks darting out on a major adventure and back beneath Mum, Tilly was at her best. She soon became tired of the small run and began pacing up and down the length of the run looking for a way out, occasionally bowling an unwary chick over as she became more and more frustrated. She had frequent visitors to the run and permitted viewing from a distance but there was an invisible boundary inches from the wire where it was clear they were not welcome.

After two weeks the chicks were also keen for freedom so the run was opened and Tilly and her gang sallied forth. The days passed and the chicks were growing well, scratching and pecking and wandering in the sun. These were happy times.

We knew about the kitten across the road. Cats, five behind, two up the road and three opposite, surround our house. We rarely saw a cat on our property and certainly never near our hens. The kitten, which belonged to Neil who lived a few houses down the road on the opposite side, was light grey with a white patch down his throat. The kitten was much loved. The kitten quickly did what kittens do – became a cat. We were aware of his occasional presence in the garden and more than once he had been chased off but he began to be spotted in the field at the bottom of the garden early in the mornings.

Each day Tilly and her chicks would be released from their run before breakfast. They would stay in the garden for the first hour, before moving further afield later. Monday evening we noticed a chick was missing and another had vanished by lunchtime on Tuesday. Wednesday, Tilly and the remaining chicks vanished soon after being released and despite a frantic search did not reappear until bedtime but minus another chick. Thursday, Tilly and remaining chicks were kept locked in the run. We had no idea where, when or how the chicks had gone missing. Friday and the weekend the lock-up continued. The cat was spotted on top of the run but scarpered once we shouted at it. That was the first clue.

On the Monday Tilly and the chicks were released and a close check was kept on her for the first hour. Whilst shaving, a huge din was heard in the garden. Rushing to the window I could see the chicks had scattered across the garden and Tilly was clucking away in great distress. A head count revealed another chick missing. The following morning, Tilly was released but a watch was kept with loaded air rifle from the bedroom window. Ten minutes after they were released, the grey cat was spotted conducting a stealthy approach towards the chicks using the shed as cover. Armed with the rifle, the window open, a clear shot was possible at the cat. The rifle was accurate but not equipped with telescopic sights. Aiming a foot in front of the cat at a piece of wood, the pellet struck home and the cat froze for a second and then fled.

The next few days passed peacefully but the following weekend, whilst standing watch, a blur of grey was seen darting out from behind the shed. The cat had the chick in a second and was back behind cover before the rifle could be poked out of the window. Frustrated with an inadequate speed of reaction the chase began. Tearing downstairs, I flew into the street watching for the cat crossing the road. As I reached for a stone, the grey monster cantered across the road, chick in mouth and but as I drew back the throwing arm it took cover behind a car.

We now had the villain, the time, the modus operandi and an arrest or worse was contemplated. We decided the cat had breakfasted on bantam chick for the last time. Again Tilly and the three remaining chicks were behind bars. The cat, spotted occasionally, was deterred with the odd stone.

Thinking we had lost the battle but determined to win the war, Tilly and the chicks were confined for a week. Tilly still demanded her freedom, pacing the wire in a demented manner all day so we thought supervised liberty was once again in order. Supervision was conducted between washing, shaving and dressing. Two days went by with no trouble. The third day, mid shave, the dreadful squawking in the garden began. Dashing to the window, the cat, with chick in mouth and head held high was advancing at a steady trot down the garden path. In shock at the arrogance of it all, the rifle remained unloaded and the window was a struggle to open. Too late the cat and its breakfast had gone. Dressing quickly I left the house and strode across the road and knocked on the cat owner's door expecting to remonstrate with Neil. Instead it was his brother who answered, Neil being away, and having been given a brief history of the bantam saga and asked to pass a clinical message to Neil involving a rifle, new telescopic sights and a cat, I returned home.

That evening, telescopic sights having been bought, fitted, zeroed and tested in the garden at various ranges, Neil came to the door. He was tired and emotional with quivering bottom lip and full of 'You can't shoot the cat, it's against the law'. Invited in to see the scene of the cat crime, we passed the rifle lying on the kitchen table and I relished pointing it out to him as we went up the steps to the garden. We spent 15 minutes discussing the pros and cons of cats vis à vis hens and he left with an assurance I would not shoot the cat but would scare it off and he promised to keep the cat in the house until after breakfast time.

The two remaining chicks survived and are now good layers. The cat has matured and cannot take fully grown bantams, Neil is a friend again and the rifle is only used against crows, pigeons and rabbits.

FEARLESS COCKERELS by CHRIS HYDE

Whilst working in London, it meant early starts each and every business working day. The first job of every day was the animals. In order to sort the chickens out this required a short walk to the barns to distribute some corn and pellets, dressed in nothing more than a dressing gown. During this time my chickens, two cocks (one of which was an enormous speckled affair) and six hens, were completely free, roaming and scrapping wherever they wished. My morning ritual was therefore simple; firstly let my dog out, whistle for the chickens then over to the barn for food scattering.

The normal scene would be: one dog heading off into the woods to do what dogs do first thing in the morning and eight chickens around my ankles and calves patiently waiting for

me to open the padlocked barn door to obtain their food. Now Duke, my dog, a 120lb German Shepherd, knew he was not allowed near any of the chickens, and as he had grown up with this rule he was generally quite good.

On one particular morning when slightly behind my schedule, I was just in the process of unlocking the barn, when suddenly I felt this scraping down the back of one of my calves. I turned round to see the speckled cockerel lining up for another go. So I raised my foot to stop the talons drawing more blood, but the cockerel kept on attacking. I even tried a Johnny Wilkinson drop goal on the cockerel, but still it kept on attacking, fluttering its wings and kicking out with both talons. What could I do? I was late for work and pinned in by a cockerel. It then came to me in a flash of inspiration, call Duke. I shouted his name and he came running out of the woods like the proverbial cavalry. To my amazement though, he came and sat right next to me and watched the cockerel's next attack. I suggested to him that he might like to sort this situation out by asserting his authority. His head turned, he looked at me as if to say: "Are you sure about this, are you really asking me to stamp my authority on one of the chickens I'm not supposed to go anywhere near?" My answer was a resounding "YES". At which point Duke's eyes lit up and the cockerel wished it had vertical take-off capabilities. The following chase was hilarious, the cockerel zigzagging his way down the paddock chortling to himself with Duke in hot pursuit and about 18 inches from his tail feathers. All ended amicably with the cockerel taking refuge in a tree and Duke sitting beneath, waiting patiently.

DIRTY EGGS by CHRIS HYDE

Some friends from London came to stay with their two children, Alex 6 years and Ellie 8 years. The big excitement for the weekend was going to be breakfast on the Sunday morning, with fresh home-cooked bread and free-range scrambled eggs with salmon. The morning arrived, so I asked Alex and Ellie to go out to the chicken house and collect the newly laid eggs, which they duly did. By now the rest of us were sitting round the kitchen table drinking tea, waiting for the children to return.

After about 15 minutes, they returned, looking most upset. They presented me with six freshly laid eggs, covered in what free-range eggs get covered in. They then explained to everyone in the kitchen they could not possibly eat the eggs they had just collected as they were not real eggs because real eggs are totally clean and come in a box.

GLOSSARY

Air Space, sac or cell
The air space at the broad end of the egg which expands with age or in a fertile egg provides the chick with air before hatching.

Ark
Portable hen house with slatted floor.

Autosexing
Method by which chicks can be sexed when they hatch by the colour of their down.

Barring
Alternative strips of two distinct colours across the feathers.

Blastoderm (Germinal Disc or Blastodisc)
The germ in a fertile egg identified as a spot in the yolk.

Blood Spots
The spots of blood formed on the yolk of an egg which are caused by the rupture of small blood vessels during the formation of the egg.

Bumblefoot
A swollen lump on the foot which could be caused by jumping off high perches.

Candling
Examining an egg under bright light in order to look at its interior, usually to see if it is fertilised.

Chalazae
Stringy bands of protein which hold the yolk in place inside the white.

China or Crock Eggs
'Pretend' eggs used to encourage hens to lay in a particular nest or to test for broodiness.

Crest
A tuft of feathers over the head of a few breeds such as the Araucana and Houdan.

Cuckoo
Cuckoo Barring is a term for colouring where two colours running across the feathers are not distinctive and merge into each other. A good example is the Cuckoo Maran.

Deep Litter
Floor covering, usually of straw, which is allowed to build up with fresh layers put on top of old ones for one or two years before being removed.

Down
The covering of hair on baby chicks sometimes referred to as fluff.

Dust Bath
A bath of fine dust, earth, ash or sand, which the bird uses to clean herself and which helps remove parasites.

Ear Lobes
The flesh seen just below the ears. Lobes differ in colour, shape and size. Hens with white ear lobes generally lay white eggs.

Egg Binding
Blockage of oviduct by extra large egg.

Egg Tooth
The hard horny tip on a newly hatched chick's beak used for chipping its way out of the shell. It falls off later.

Feathered Legs
Feathers cover the legs of the bird as in breeds such as Brahma, Cochin, Pekin and Faverolle.

Frizzled
A term used for curled feathers as in the Frizzle breed.

Gizzard
A part of the hen's digestive system where food gets ground up with the help of grit.

Hackles
The narrow, long and pointed feathers which grow on the neck. Those on the back of a cock are called saddle hackles.

Heavy Breed
A classification of breed which was originally connected to the Cochin and Brahma. The hen should average more than 2.5kilos and examples of heavy breeds are Rhode Island Reds and Light Sussex.

Hybrid
A modern term used for the scientific breeding of commercial poultry.

In-Breeding
The mating of closely related birds, not to be recommended.

Lacing
Feather marking in which edging is of a different colour to the inside of the feather.

Light Breed
Breeds which are light and quick feathering but more flighty than heavy breeds.

Mottling
Feather marking where there are spots of a different colour at the end of the feather.

Muffled
An abundance of feathers on each side of the face.

Non Sitters
Non sitters are breeds which do not go broody and tend therefore to lay more eggs and include Ancona, Welsummer, Leghorn, Minorca, Hamburgh and Poland.

Oviduct
Long tube where egg formation takes place which leads from the ovary to the cloaca.

Pea Comb
A triple comb which resembles three single combs joined together.

Pencilling
Small markings of stripes across the feather as in the Hamburgh or concentric in form following the outline of the feather as in the silver pencilled Wyandotte.

Point of Lay (POL)
Pullets which are about to lay their first egg.

Pullet
A young female bird of 12 months or less.

Rose Comb
A broad flat comb covered with small points.

Single Comb
Traditional comb with single upright blade, serrated like a saw.

Sitters
Breeds such as Orpington, Plymouth Rock, Rhode Island Red, Maran, Wyandotte, Sussex and Dorking are all sitters which means they go broody and sit easily.

Spangling
Large spots of colour on the feathers different from the ground colour.

Spur
A horny substance growing from the shanks of the cock near the heel. Occasionally hens will develop spurs.

Triple Comb - *see Pea Comb*

Uterus
Part of the female reproduction system where the shell is produced.

Wattles
The flesh-like skin at each side of the base of the beak, chiefly developed in the cock.

USEFUL ADDRESSES AND WEBSITES

The Domestic Fowl Trust and Honeybourne Rare Breeds
Station Road, Honeybourne,
Nr Evesham, Worcs WR11 7QZ   www.domesticfowltrust.co.uk

The Poultry Club, 30 Grosvenor Rd,
Frampton, Boston, Lincs PE20 1DB   www.poultryclub.org

Kintaline Poultry and Waterfowl Centre   www.kintaline.co.uk

Ascott Smallholding Supplies Ltd   www.ascott.biz

P & T Poultry   www.pandtpoultry.co.uk

Bobkan Poultry   www.bobkan.co.uk
Bedfordshire   Agents of Black Rock Hybrids

The Good Life Poultry Company   www.goodlifepoultry.co.uk
sells hybrids

Garden Poultry   www.gardenpoultry.cwc.net
sells pure breeds

Devonshire Traditional Breed Centre   www.dtbcentre.co.uk

Belton Quality One Stop Chicken Shop & Poultry Centre Tel: 01476 566057

Country Smallholding Magazine, Fair Oak Close,
Exeter Airport Business Park, Clyst Honiton,
Exeter, Devon EX5 2UL   www.countrysmallholding.co.uk

The Smallholder, Hook House, Wimblington, March,
Cambs PE15 OQL   www.smallholder.co.uk

Breeders whose hens feature in the colour section
Foxfield Fowls   Clair Housden
Foxfield House   Vineyard Lodge
Narrow Lane,   Saffron Walden
Ringwood, Hants BH24 3EN   Essex

Index

W

Y

Z